PWomen of Prayer

Released to the Nations

Sixteen prayer leaders around the earth
reveal the heart, spirit, and power of prayer.

AGLOW

A Ministry of Women's Aglow Fellowship, Int'l.
P.O. Box 1548
Lynnwood, WA 98046-1548
USA

Cover design by Paz Design Group

Suggested Subject Heading: Prayer/Christian Living

Women's Aglow Fellowship, International, is a nondenominational organization of Christian women. Our mission is to lead women to Jesus Christ and provide opportunity for Christian women to grow in their faith and minister to others.

Our publications are used to help women find a personal relationship with Jesus Christ, to enhance growth in their Christian experience, and to help them recognize their roles and relationship according to Scripture.

For more information about Women's Aglow Fellowship, please write to Women's Aglow Fellowship, Int'l., P.O. Box 1548, Lynnwood, WA 98046-1548, USA, or call (206) 775-7282.

Unless otherwise noted, all scripture quotations in this publication are from the Holy Bible, New King James Version. Copyright © 1979, 1980, 1982, Thomas Nelson, Inc. Other versions abbreviated as follows: NCV (New Century Version), NIV (New International Version), TAB (The Amplified Bible), TLB (The Living Bible).

ISBN 1-56616-004-9

1 2 3 4 5 6 7 8 9 10 Printing / Year 97 96 95 94 93

Dedicated to our Aglow sisters
throughout the world:
as you pray, you share
the heart of God
for the nations

Contents

Introduction

Aglow women have always been people of prayer.

Since Women's Aglow Fellowship, International, (WAFI) began in 1967 in Seattle, Washington, U.S.A., members have sought the Father's presence as they helped others to know Jesus Christ as their personal Savior, and discipled them into maturity.

More than a quarter of a century later, this nondenominational "network of caring women" is ministering in 110 nations around the world from Australia to Alaska, U.S.A., from Ghana to Germany to Guatemala.

This book is a record of the power of God's movement among His people throughout the earth. It is a testimony told by Aglow leaders from five continents. They would be the first to say they are ordinary women, touched by the Father's grace to witness His loving sovereignty, often in impossible circumstances.

Listen to Lisha Land from the Netherlands share her prison experience during World War II: "Day after day, I sat alone in my cell while fear gripped my heart. Would the German police question me again until deep in the night, as they had done that first evening? Would I be able to keep calm? Would there be torture? Starvation? Fear lay like a brick at the pit of my stomach. I knew only one way to battle fear and that was prayer."

Christiana Darko from Ghana, Africa, gives us a down-to-earth lesson about waiting on the Lord in prayer: "As a director of our family poultry business . . . I have learned that it always takes twenty-one days for a chicken to hatch from the egg. We cannot speed up the process; otherwise, we will have a stillborn chick."

Marfa Cabrera, from Argentina reveals this about fasting and praying: "Fasting with prayer is a place where God can cause a change to occur in us; we place ourselves where God's blessings can reach us."

We are given unique perspectives on how to pray, with biblical studies by Joan Morton, Australia; Susan Goodnight, Pat Chen and Cindy Jacobs, U.S.A.

We step into Siberia as Doris Ott shows us the Holy Spirit's work there and in countries from the former U.S.S.R. We get an intimate look at the Muslim woman as Iqbal Massey pulls aside the veil to reveal her mind and heart.

We receive teaching on healing prayer, persevering (soaking) prayer, prophetic prayer, receiving a prayer burden, praying for our families, each written by a leader who has lived it, and ministered it.

8

Women of Prayer is divided into three sections. Section I, "Called into the Father's Presence," allows us to hear about the heart of prayer; Section II, "Called to the Nations," draws us to the spirit of prayer; Section III, "Released to the Nations," shows us the power of prayer.

Preceding each chapter is a short biography of its Aglow leader/author, to better acquaint you with her background, and her heart for Aglow.

"Aglow will be a network of praying, warring, interceding women, covering the face of the earth," was the message International President Jane Hansen heard from the Lord in 1980. She shares her stirring vision for the future of Aglow in the final chapter.

This book has been prayed into existence. It stands as part of God's wondrous heritage for us. Be enriched. Be challenged. Be blessed. Thank the Father for His gift.

Section I

Called into the Father's Presence

The Heart of Prayer

SUSAN I. GOODNIGHT

Former Vice-president and Publisher of Aglow Publications Susan I. Goodnight combined vision, a thorough knowledge of Aglow fellowships, and business expertise to create a "tentmaking" endeavor for Women's Aglow Fellowship, International.

Susan's thirteen years in Aglow provided a leadership backdrop for her position as publisher. She has served as an Aglow local president; vice-president of retreats, area board; vice-president of leadership, area board; president, area board.

Susan's move across the United States in 1987 to join the Aglow international headquarters staff in Seattle, Washington, as publisher was made only after weeks of prayer. She remembers that she cried out to God about leaving her home, her relatives, her career, and lifelong friendships in upstate New York. "The Lord impressed on me that if I'd give those things up, He'd give me a pen that would write around the world," she says. When the publications department began selling subsidiary rights to our books in other nations, that began to come true."

1

...

Humility in Intercession: Esther's Story

By Susan I. Goodnight

"The sure way to be humble is not to stoop until you are smaller than yourself, but to stand at your real height against some higher nature that will show you what the real smallness of your greatness is. Stand at your highest, and then look at Christ, then go away and forever be humble." So remarked the great American preacher, Phillip Brooks.

Everything in life needs a plumb line by which it can be measured. As praying Christians, the more clearly we see God's greatness, the easier it is to humble ourselves before Him in the absolute certainly that without Him all is lost. Until then, most likely we will not understand true humility.

Esther's Story

I have a notion that somewhere along the path in young Esther's life journey, as recorded in the Bible, she had to come to that revelation of the awesomeness of God.

Ironically, Esther had been chosen queen in Babylon, the land of her captivity. She had been called to the kingdom for this very time: the fate of the Hebrew nation rested upon what had been worked into her heart. Hers would be the voice used to come against the evil intent of Haman, the most honored nobleman of King Ahasuerus' court.

Maybe Esther's certainty of God's greatness came when she was praying and fasting. Perhaps it was when she resolved to do what she had to do when she finalized her decision with, "and if I perish, I perish" (Esther 4:16). At some precise moment the eye of faith saw more clearly and profoundly than ever before. Somewhere in her spirit she saw the majesty of God. Only then was she able to put away all false humility—the motions of crouching and stooping that we as humans do to appear humble.

I can see her, regal and beautiful, standing at her highest, looking to Yahweh and realizing the smallness of her greatness, then moving on—greatly humbled—but prepared for the task set before her, the task of saving a nation.

The Spirit of Pride

In Babylon, the spirit of pride, self-centeredness, and self-exultation was once again the vehicle of malice trying to destroy God's people.

Pride was the reason for Haman's scheme. He heard about Mordecai, the devout Jew, who sat within the gate of the king, the one who refused to bow as Haman passed.

Mordecai knew that bowing down in undue honor to some-one is a form of idolatry, and thus unacceptable to God. For him there was no other choice. Haman was an Agagite, a descendant of the Amalekites, staunch enemies of God.

Pride is a hard task master. It provokes and prods desperate men to desperate solutions. Infuriated by this man's unwillingness to honor him, Haman determined to destroy the whole Hebrew nation. Pride provoked him to convince the king that there was justice in his hideous scheme of trying Mordecai for treason and exterminating a people.

Using his position to maximum advantage, Haman told the king that the Jews were despicable vagabonds, that they were dangerous, having their own laws and not conforming to the laws of the kingdom. With slanderous accusations and 10,000 talents of silver, Haman succeeded in obtaining a decree whereby all Jewish men, women, and children would be massacred in one day and their goods plundered.

I wonder if at some point if Mordecai's trial for treason didn't seem a bit ludicrous to Esther. Why after all would one man so zealously try to convince the king that an entire nation of people be eliminated? Such arrogance.

But pride has a life of its own; it is an insatiable self-serving goad. It drives and warps the heart to the place of obsession. Turning its venom outward, pride lures the dissatisfied, the fearful, and the angry. Its goal: to reproduce itself in enough hearts that its sheer strength in numbers brings a measure of credibility to its irrational existence.

Satan's Pride

Satan, loving his own beauty, fell into pride and self-centeredness. Five times he addressed himself against God, with his "I will" proclamations. "I will ascend into heaven, I will exalt my throne above the stars of God; I will also sit on the mount of the congregation . . .; I will ascend above the heights of the clouds . . .," and finally, "I will be like the Most High" (Isa. 14:13-14). Then he, too, took his case beyond himself—to a woman—to convince her of the rationality of his plan.

He represented God to Eve in a very wrong way. She allied herself with his pride-based lies. Because she did not come into Satan's presence in the opposite spirit of humility and truth that she had experienced with God, the world was to be forever changed.

Warfare with a Humble Spirit

In proud Babylon, for Esther to stand against the very power of hell itself, intercession from a humbled heart was of the utmost importance. Did she have the strength to come to this appointment with the spirit opposite to that of the enemy's—the spirit of humility?

She was, after all, a prisoner of war, a child without parents, one not born into position. Her sudden change of life, power, and prestige must have been overwhelming.

It was Esther's beauty, not her character, that initially brought her favor with the king and caused him to choose her. Before that she was insignificant, a captive in a foreign land. There is no mention of any great prophecy that had been spoken over her by the elders of that day, but the anointing on her inner and outer beauty propelled her to that place of power.

Would she put aside her newly acquired throne? Could she be obedient and not panic in the face of great danger— perhaps death? Could she withhold her true identity until that moment when, with the verbal deftness of an experienced diplomat, she would speak the words that would convict the guilty, exonerate the innocent?

We sing the chorus, "The victory is mine when the battle is the Lord's. . . ." but unless we have seen the Lord high and lifted up, powerful and mighty, we cannot lay aside our own abilities long enough to engage in the battle the Lord's way, to lay down our swords, and throw the fateful stone that will slay the giant.

But God, who knows the hearts of men, had already provided for the deliverance of His people. He provided one who would come in the opposite spirit, one who would come in meekness and humility in prayer and intercession.

At the instruction of Mordecai, her adoptive parent, the young queen began her task of interceding for her people with prayer and fasting, passing through the fears, the whys, the inner tremblings.

God's Hand on Mordecai

During this time, Mordecai was also being positioned by God. While at the royal gate, he had heard of a treasonous plot to kill the king. Using Esther to warn her husband, Mordecai helped to cement her position with him as a loyal, loving wife and recommended himself as a loyal subject whose name was put in a special book of remembrance.

By the time Haman's plan unfolded, God's praying intercessors were in place.

The Place of Captivity

The news of Haman's plan spread quickly. Fear gripped the Hebrew people. Wasn't it enough that they had been taken by force from their homeland? Were they all to die in the midst of their captivity?

We forget that Satan will always bring us to a place of captivity of some sort before trying to work the final destruction.

Jesus stated emphatically that He is the way, the truth, and the life (John 14:6), in direct opposition to Satan's captive-making snares. Jesus would have us enslaved to nothing. If we know the truth that He, being the Truth, will set us free, why are some of us held captive?

Captivity is a strange phenomenon. We accept the life style of bondage because there's a peculiar security we feel when we know our boundaries in the daily performances of life. There is a same-old, same-old about captivity that masquerades as safety. Although it's suffocating and morally wrong, it can become comfortable in a morbid sort of way. That is why the question of choice always remains critical at a time like this.

Freedom Is a Choice

Choice was a critical question for Queen Esther.

It has to be more than a cause that carries leadership into these waters. It has to be relationship, a bond that umbilically ties the one whose choice it is, to someone far larger and more magnificent than oneself.

Humility always springs from the consciousness of God's greatness.

For Mordecai, the choice was clear because his life of relationship had been consistent. Mordecai knew his God. He humbly postured himself before the Lord crying bitterly, rending his clothes, and putting on sackcloth and ashes.

Esther and all the Jews fasted and prayed as well. Weakened in body, humbled before God, that excellent spirit was released. Esther knew God intended that she be a major part in the attempted deliverance of her people.

Confusion of Purpose

Some believe humility in prayer and fasting is little more than a foolish exercise, certainly a course of very little "real" action in the face of such great and imminent danger. It is true that this course boasts very little worldly wisdom, but this was not a worldly war.

In the spiritual realm the war rages with principalities and powers being thwarted and toppled.

Esther went to the king's courtyard trusting in the King of Kings. The spirit of humility in intercession effectively destroyed any idol that may have enticed her as she advanced toward her royal position. Scripture makes it very clear: "The fear of the Lord is to hate evil; pride and arrogance and the evil way" (Prov. 8:13). God, her God and ours, does not forget the cry of the humble. Humility in prayer not only cries out to God for mercy; it releases the power of God in a moment's time to deliver from the evil one. When we hold nothing back from God, He is free to grant us everything.

Bold in her meekness, Esther approached her husband's courtyard, walking delicately along the edge of life and death.

As Esther was recognized, King Ahasuerus extended the golden scepter and encouraged her to speak. Esther asked the king and Haman to attend one banquet and then a second. Each time, the king asked Esther to voice any request she might desire of him, even to the half of his kingdom. But Esther's needs were far beyond properties and position.

Haman's pride at being included in these banquets knew no bounds. And with that artificial state of invincibility, other aspects of his character became more pronounced: impatience, revenge, contempt, dominion at its most detestable. He fantasized about his singular relationship with the king and queen. He no longer had a need to stay his revenge on Mordecai, whose refusal to bow struck at Haman's insatiable pride. By now, Haman was above all that; he could get on with the business of murder.

With a little help from Haman's wife and friends, a plan was devised. Mordecai would be hanged from a tall scaffolding.

God's Sovereignty in the Situation

But even as they schemed, God caused the king to be restless and unable to sleep. One night, as a scribe read to Ahasuerus from the royal book of remembrance, they came upon the heroic deeds of Mordecai. Since nothing had been done to honor him the king gave careful and lengthy thought to correcting this oversight.

The next day Haman went to the palace confident that he lived in a world insulated from harm. The king, still considering the tribute to be paid to Mordecai, asked Haman how best to honor someone truly deserving. Blinded by pride, Haman was convinced the king was about to pay him another tribute. Not knowing that he meant the honor for Mordecai, Haman suggested the king bestow the highest favor possible.

Pride's Reward

Pride had dealt Haman the first of two deadly blows. The first was to come as soon as the words left his lips: "Let a royal robe be brought which the king has worn, and a horse on which the king has ridden, which has a royal crest placed on his head. . . . Then parade him on horseback through the city square, and proclaim before him: 'Thus shall it be done to the man whom the king delights to honor!' " (Esther 6:8-9).

The king replied, " 'As you have suggested . . . *do so for Mordecai*, the Jew who sits within the king's gate. Leave nothing undone of all that you have spoken' " (Esther 6:10).

Imagine the assault to Haman's mind and emotions. He

was but moments away from having this man hanged, and now he would be the one to confer eminent recognition upon him.

As commanded, Haman personally placed the royal robe upon Mordecai, presented him with a horse the king had previously ridden, and led him through the city square.

The Final Banquet

At the banquet, the king for the third time asks Esther to make her request. The time is precisely right. She asks for her life and the life of her people. Pride's second deadly blow is struck as Haman is identified as the man who would annihilate a nation.

On that very day, the king gave Esther the house of Haman. Mordecai was given Haman's signet ring, symbol of governing power. Now he would have his enemy's position and property. Haman would hang on the gallows prepared for Mordecai.

For a leader who had never profoundly experienced relationship with God Almighty, the story may well have ended here. But for Esther, the final proclamation had not yet been made. The curse had not yet been lifted from all her people.

Esther fell down at the king's feet and begged him with tearful pleadings to undo what Haman had done.

There is great significance to this action. Humility often ends when the crisis subsides. The commonplace is to stand up in our own power and wisdom when we feel safe once more. But even from her powerful advantage, the worst seemingly over, Esther maintained her posture of humility waiting for the scepter to be extended to her yet again.

Not only did King Ahasuerus allow the decree of Haman to be rescinded, he allowed Esther to write the decree as she saw fit. She was given power of attorney to use the king's name and seal. Thus the words of life were spread through all the land in the script and language of the people. Not only was the curse reversed, but the people were released to protect themselves from their enemies and plunder their spoils.

When leadership comes in the spirit of humility in intercession—in the opposite spirit of the enemy—there is a release from heaven that filters through all the people and brings health, safety, and deliverance. So great was the Babylonians' fear of the Jews and awe of their God because of this incredible turn of events, many willingly became believers.

Our Access to the King

Our opportunity is so different from Esther's: the law was tenuous and restrictive to Esther; grace is extended freely to us. We are instructed in Hebrews to come boldly before the throne of grace. We don't need to wait for a golden scepter to be extended. God's word is always "come." "Come to me all you. . . ." (Matt. 11:28). "The Spirit and the bride say, come!" (Rev. 22:17).

The Work of Jesus in Us

The more we experience God the more we will understand and thrive humbly before Him. The less we will feign humility; the less we will be satisfied with the lower place so that we might be invited to the higher one.

There is no groveling spirit in the heart of the truly humble.

We may do hard things, fight hard battles, but we will know our limitations and accept them. We will operate from a different heart and from a spirit that is not agitated and hasty.

24

Apart from the work of Jesus in us, this kind of humility cannot be accomplished. Humility in Jesus flies in the face of the norm that has been earth's sentence since the fall. It's no wonder that we will be different, that we are constantly being changed into His image, an image from above, not born of personal human striving. The world doesn't have time for such humility because godly humanity has no self-serving qualities to it.

"As Far As the Altars"

This kind of humility in prayer follows an old Babylonian saying *usque ad aras* meaning "as far as the altars." For the ancients of Esther's and Daniel's day, this simply meant that people might live and work effectively in a society not of their own choosing, but when it came to prayer and intercession, worship and obedience, they parted company with the existing world and bowed the knee and heart to God alone.

The humble intercessor knows that she cannot understand life or death without God's help. As Isaiah 57:15 assures us, God Himself dwells with the contrite and humble spirit. James tells us that He resists the proud. The heavens are continually closed to the arrogant.

The haughty, God knows at a distance, but the humble He knows intimately and greatly respects. The intercessor who comes before God in this manner will not only arise forever changed, but may, in the process, change the course of a nation's history.

BOBBYE BYERLY

"The key to my prayer life is intimacy with God; I arise early each morning for time alone with Him," says Bobbye Byerly, Aglow's new vice-president of prayer and evangelism.

She has served on Aglow's International Prayer Council, represented Aglow as their international prayer representative, and functioned on Aglow's United States board.

Bobbye became a charter member of the first Aglow fellowship in New Orleans, Louisiana, in 1977. That year, she served as its vice-president and then president. In 1980 she accepted a term as statewide Aglow president.

Bobbye spent one of her most profound times in prayer during the time she and her husband served on the prayer team at the 1989 Lausanne Conference in the Philippines. God broke into her prayers at 4 A.M. "He spoke deeply in my heart that He had strategically placed Aglow in the earth at this time to bring forth a movement of prayer in the nations of the world. This prayer would be a vital part of the fulfillment of the Great Commission and would result in a mass end-time global harvest."

2

...

How to Receive
a Burden from God

By Bobbye Byerly

Take My yoke upon you and learn from Me, for I am
gentle and lowly in heart, and you will find rest for
your souls. For My yoke is easy and My burden is
light (Matt. 11:29-30).

Because only the Holy Spirit can reveal the Father's
heart, the very first step in receiving a burden from God is
to get to know Him. I am convinced that there are no
shortcuts or simple steps toward receiving the burden of
God in prayer.

The Father yearns for us to share His heart by spending
time in His presence. The next step is to know it is a
process that builds His purpose in us when we consistently

29

spend time before Him. It is a priority because faithfulness in prayer builds confidence in prayer.

As the Holy Spirit reveals what Jesus, our great intercessor, is praying, we can join Him in His prayers. He wants our hearts to beat with His. He longs to share our nights and days. He will not withhold His plans and purposes from his friends.

As I study the prayer life of Jesus, I see the priority prayer had in His life. He always sought to do the will of His Father. His desire was that God would receive glory in everything He did. He spent busy days in ministry and then long nights in prayer. Jesus worked in the midst of pressure but was never pressured.

Before every decision in His earthly ministry, He sought God's will, way, and purpose. Jesus received the burden from His Father. His disciples saw the effectiveness of His time spent with His Father, and one cried out, "Lord, teach us to pray" (Luke 11:1).

A Passion for God

I love partnering with Jesus in His intercession. My favorite time each day is spent alone in sweet communion with God. The Holy Spirit has worked within me to give me a passion for God, a heart for unity in His Body, and a burden for the lost in our world.

Prayer is a privilege God has granted us. He limits Himself to our praying, then He releases His greatness in the earth. One key to praying is humility. With Jesus, our desire must be that God receive all the glory.

Studying the holy Word of God over the past thirty years has been such a rich experience in my life. The more I read and study about God the more intrigued with Him I become. It is not just reading the Bible that gives me life, but it is getting to know the Author of the Bible. The more intimately acquainted with Him I become, the more I desire to know Him even more deeply.

Everything about God intrigues me. I cannot get enough of God.

His Burden for Our Loved Ones

Two stories from my own life have helped me to keep praying and keep my heart united with God's, even when I don't see the results.

I prayed for more than fifteen years to have my mother healed. She was labeled a manic depressive, with multiple addictions. One day, I voiced my thoughts aloud to God, "Hers is such a wasted life."

From deep within I sensed a response from God, "Whatever I have given breath to, don't you call wasted." I was stunned, but my gaze was turned immediately from our creature-weaknesses to God, the Creator, and all His strength.

About four months later, my mother accepted Christ as her Lord and Savior. She was instantaneously delivered from darkness, the bondages of her depression and addictions were broken, and she was restored to life. The strong arm of God was displayed in her behalf.

God is a covenant-keeping God. I know many had been burdened for years to pray for her, and God miraculously set her free.

In further testimony of His faithfulness, my entire family has been birthed into the kingdom of God. We now walk as a family in His covenant promises.

God's Covenant/My Life

I was raised in a mixed denominational family: my mother was Catholic, my father was Protestant.

My mother's mother, Nana, was the greatest Christian

influence in my early life. She was a devout Catholic and a strict disciplinarian; I learned a reverence for God from her and from the Catholic church, and I was taught to love and respect Protestantism. It seems as if I have always known that God deeply loves His Church. He said He would build His Church and the gates of hell would not prevail against it. He has a deep desire for the people in His Church to come into harmony with Himself and one another.

My father and his father, as well as his sisters and brother and their spouses, also helped raise me and greatly influenced my life as well. My mother spent the first twenty-seven years of my life in and out of mental hospitals.

God does chasten the ones He loves. He disciplines His children. I am no exception. God has always led me even when I did not know or recognize His leading. He was working in my life all the time giving me a love for Himself and a deep desire for unity in His body.

Our Inner Wounds Healed

When I met and fell in love with Jim at eighteen, we were married in the Protestant church. Jim and I began our shared life forty-two years ago. I can count it all joy now, but that was not always true. I brought into my marriage all the wounds and hurts of my childhood. Combining my husband's wounds and hurts with mine, we started out on a shaky road. We began our family, and by the time we celebrated our tenth wedding anniversary we had three wonderful sons. We both deeply loved one another—at least we thought we did.

Things looked good on the outside. From surface appearances we were an ideal, church-going family. My husband was climbing the ladder of success in his career. I had always desired to be a loving wife and a good mother. I was at home, enjoying caring for our children. As I look back now, in many ways we were a blessed family.

Yet, my blessings were no longer blessing me. I tried hard, but gradually, the very things I longed to be, were slipping out of my grasp. It seemed as if my love just leaked out. It did not flow freely to those I loved.

I was a woman bent out of shape. In desperation over my failing marriage, I cried out to God.

A Death and a Challenge

Then my father died. I felt even more lost.

As I flew from New Jersey to Texas to attend his funeral, a Japanese man seated next to me sensed I was deeply troubled. He began trying to draw me out, but I felt trapped by his questions. In fact, I felt he was intruding where he had no right. I tried to politely put him in his place, but he was not deterred.

He kept saying, "Lady, you are deeply troubled."

Finally, I blurted out that I was enroute to my father's funeral. He was silent for a moment. Then he asked a penetrating question, "Do you know my Jesus?"

I responded that I had been in church all my life.

He asked a second time, "Do you know my Jesus?"

Grieving, confused, frustrated, I turned away and looked out the window.

Set Free

When I returned home after the funeral, Jim had no idea how empty and lonely I felt. I had learned for many years not to express my feelings, thinking they were a sign of weakness. I had really needed Jim with me in Houston but had not asked him to accompany me.

In desperation, I went to my pastor. He counseled me for several weeks, but nothing seemed to help. Over the next six weeks I grew more and more desperate.

Women of Prayer

Finally one day in his office during a counseling session, I just blurted out the question the Japanese man had asked me, "Do you know my Jesus?" To my utter amazement, suddenly I was in the holy presence of God.

I was crying and surrendering my life to Him all at the same time. I saw myself a sinner in need of a Savior and He was there saving me. I began literally unloading everything that had been locked up inside me for years. The tenderness of God overwhelmed me. I was crying but I did not feel condemned. To the contrary—I was being set free.

My encounter that marvelous day with the living Lord was for all time to change my life. I walked into that office a woman desperately bent out of shape; I came out a new creation with the love of God shed abroad in my heart. No longer would the statement, "I have been in church all my life," rule me, because now I knew Jesus Christ as my Lord and Savior.

Be Willing

I'm sure you are asking at this point, how does this give you a burden from God?

That is exactly the process: It is God who changes us. We are helpless to change ourselves. "But we all, with unveiled face, beholding as in a mirror the glory of the Lord, are being transformed into the same image from glory to glory, just as by the Spirit of the Lord" (2 Cor. 3:18). He only asks that we be willing.

Radiating Change

Experiencing Christ in this dimension caused me to fall in love with Jim all over again, only this time our marriage was built on a firm foundation. My relationships within my family were changed. I began to see the glorious transforming power of God in my home and all about me.

34

I developed a hunger for the Word of God. I studied and began going to Bible studies and prayer meetings. I was allowing God to adjust me—get me off the center of myself, unto Himself. I was trying now to be a good Christian, and it was painful.

God is ever faithful to Himself and so patient with us. He continually gives us fresh new beginnings. We mess up, He fixes up and so the process goes on.

Baptism in the Holy Spirit

In 1967, six years after coming to know the Lord as my Savior, I was gloriously baptized in the Holy Spirit. With this experience God brought deeper healing to my inmost being. This revelation of God's power began transforming me afresh. I had answers to so many questions without even asking them. Daily I sought more and more of God. The Holy Spirit drew me into an intimacy I had longed for but never experienced. God began to draw me into an even deeper prayer life with His cords of love.

I had attempted through the years to discipline myself. That did not bring the same result. As I began this new experience, something was happening deep within me. I was yearning to know more about this wondrous love. I was continually being filled with the Spirit.

Getting in Stride with God

There were still problems all around me but I began seeing anointed solutions to the situations. My perspective was changing. I believe Oswald Chambers calls this getting in stride with God. The Holy Spirit was anointing my times of prayer. I was beginning to see things from God's perspective; spending time with God was a choice I made.

It is hard to put in words how I know I saw the heart of God, but I know it is the Holy Spirit's work to give revelation. Glimpses of truth encouraged and strengthened me to continue to develop a consistent prayer life.

He opened His love to me and was able to flow through me in prayer to affect the lives of others. This is not control or manipulation but the opposite—freedom to come to know God. I want to be open and vulnerable so that others may come to know the marvels of His grace. His love is deeper than all my doubts, self-centeredness, insecurity, and negative attitudes. I am free to walk in His grace. The righteousness of Jesus set me free and I am free indeed.

Proverbs 3:5-6 tells us to "trust in the Lord with all your heart, and lean not on your own understanding. In all your ways acknowledge Him, and He shall direct your paths." His love is beyond my ability to comprehend, yet I have grasped it.

After baptizing me in His Holy Spirit God began surrounding me with like-minded people. The joy of the Lord was our strength. We prayed together, shared together, and enjoyed God together.

Learning from Past Prayer Warriors

I owe a deep debt of gratitude to men and women who have authored books that have allowed me to glimpse God in new and deep ways. They have been portholes through which I have seen Christ.

Andrew Murray heads my list, followed by Watchman Nee, C. S. Lewis, Catherine Marshall, J. I. Packer, James Stott, Billy Graham, and countless others. I am so grateful to them for placing on paper life-giving experiences that have caused me to grow in Christ.

In the late sixties and early seventies I began listening to tapes of two people who also greatly impacted my life and revolutionized my prayer life, Joy Dawson and Malcolm Smith. In 1972, I heard Malcolm teach on the

Lord's Prayer and that revolutionized my entire prayer life. I gleaned more of the character of God and more of the need to pray.

I saw God's love made real in prayer through these precious saints. They helped train me to pray for the nations of the world. I began praying for spiritual awakening and revival in the eighties. Truly the light of Christ had dawned on my heart in a new way.

Praying for the nations has been my heart's cry since receiving God's burden to pray for the lost. Knowing that Jesus is the light of the world and the hope of the nations, we can, through our prayers, affect the peoples and nations of the world.

Today, I am privileged to intercede for many spiritual leaders.

Burden for a City

Jim and I moved to the greater New Orleans area in 1974. It was a new experience for me, and we lived there for seventeen years. I grew to accept New Orleans by praying for it, and later God changed acceptance to love for that city.

In 1976 while the United States of America celebrated its bicentennial, the Christians in New Orleans celebrated the Christian Spirit of '76. Audrey Kimmel and I were appointed to be co-prayer coordinators for our city. Oh, how our God inspired us to pray for our city! We received His heart for New Orleans.

In 1980, a pastor named Bill Brown, who lived in New Orleans, had a vision for a prayer movement for our city. The scripture that he felt God gave him was Jeremiah 29:7: "And seek the welfare [shalom] of the city where I have sent you into exile, and pray to the Lord on its behalf; for in its welfare [shalom] you will have welfare [shalom]"

Women of Prayer

(NAS). Our prayer movement was called "Shalom New Orleans." It swept over our city.

The Rev. Brown led us faithfully to pray for New Orleans for a decade. Jim and I both served on the steering committee for those ten wonderful years. We grew to love our city and see God move in behalf of New Orleans. Lifelong friendships were established.

Aglow in the World

In 1977, we formed the first Women's Aglow fellowship in our state. We now have at least nine active Aglows in New Orleans and twenty-eight in the state of Louisiana. We began to glimpse God's great love for women, as well as the high, holy plans He has for them.

I was so blessed in 1983 when the Aglow International Conference was held in Washington D.C. The leadership was led to have us all go out as a praying army of women and walk the streets of Washington, D.C., in Jesus' name. Thousands of women took part and I know God heard our prayers. He loves the burdened masses of people in cities.

God's heart is always burdened for the lost.

Let me share with you another illustration of praying for the lost. I went to the Philippines in July, 1989 to attend the Lausanne Congress held in Manila. There were forty-five restricted-access nations at the conference, plus people from 150 other nations. The theme of the congress was that the whole church would take the whole gospel to the world. We prayed morning, noon, and night. It was a blessed time.

My husband Jim and I were part of a team who were praying in four-hour shifts around the clock. One morning at 4 A.M. in the prayer room, I sensed the presence of God as we prayed and suddenly He broke into my prayer. This is what I heard God speaking to me: "I have strategically placed Aglow in the earth for this hour, to bring forth a global prayer thrust which will be a vital part of the mass movement of global evangelism which will fulfill the Great Commission."

I sat there shaking and crying in the presence of God. It was an awesome moment: Once again God, by his Holy Spirit, revolutionized my prayer burden for the world. One of the other intercessors asked me to share my heart, and we prayed together for God to have His will and His way in His Aglow ministry in this *kairos* (opportune) time.

God's Burden/Our Burden

All of us have witnessed the strong arm of God tearing down the Berlin Wall, unraveling communism in the re-stricted-access nations, and moving today in a global prayer thrust that is bringing the Body of Christ together.

God is vitally interested in everything that concerns us. He cares with the deepest care for our personal needs as well as those of our loved ones. He has laid hold of our hearts for Himself, that He might fulfill His highest and noblest plans for each of us and spread His marvelous light to all He brings into our lives.

We cannot afford to rest in just knowing God for our-selves, even with the wonderful blessings that we receive. We must receive His heart for the masses, to reach out and share the Good News to all the hurting people around us. May we experience His compassionate heart and see the hurting as He does.

We may only travel on our knees but we can and will bathe the earth with prayer.

We love God because He first loved us. We have been called by Him to the kingdom of His Son. We owe every-thing to Him. May we follow hard after God by choosing to receive His burden. In this way, we will daily choose life by loving the Lord our God, by clinging to Him, and by obeying His holy commandments.

Ultimately, God's plans and purposes will be fulfilled with or without us, but God also allows us to partner with Him in bringing reconciliation to this world. He will use our hearts, mouths, hands, and feet to share His love. Each of us can experience His gift of joy in our innermost being as we cooperate with God.

Jeremiah 29:11-13 are my life verses for prayer. God says "'For I know the plans that I have for you,' declares the Lord, 'plans for welfare and not for calamity to give you a future and a hope. Then you will call upon Me and come and pray to Me and I will listen to you. And you will seek Me and find Me when you search for Me with all your heart. And I will be found by you,' declares the Lord" (NAS).

My heart's cry is Psalm 25:4-5, "Show me Your ways, O Lord; teach me Your paths. Lead me in Your truth and teach me, for You are the God of my salvation, on You I wait all the day"; and Psalm 86:11, 12, "Teach me Your way O Lord; I will walk in Your truth; unite my heart to fear Your name. I will praise You, O Lord my God, with all my heart, and I will glorify Your name forever."

LISHA LAND

Lisha Land's experience with Aglow dates back to her membership on the committee that instituted the first Aglow fellowship in Holland in 1979.

Since that time, Lisha has served as president of a new fellowship in Ziest and later in Barneveld and headed training of new local boards from 1984-88. She returned to Holland's national board in 1987 where she has served as its president since 1988.

Lisha is also Aglow's field representative to the nations of Hungary and Czechoslovakia, traveling widely throughout Europe for the gospel's sake.

Early morning prayer is a must for her. "For then, every day is a new beginning with the Lord," she says.

She believes Aglow women, no matter how busy they are, should never forget to pray. "They are 'busy bees' in their household tasks, with their families, their jobs, but they turn into real women of God when they pray with Aglow vision."

3
...

How Prayer Makes a Difference

By Lisha Land

In May 1940, when I was fifteen years old, the German army marched into Holland, and the occupation of our country began. We were no longer free. World War II had begun for us.

Before the war I was still a schoolgirl. Always, I will be thankful for my happy youth and loving parents. Life didn't have many problems for me.

But the terrible events of the Second World War greatly influenced my life as a young girl. After the war I was an adult, more or less shaped by my war experience. Those years are like a dark beam in my memory.

When I finished high school in 1942, I found myself helping with various aspects of the resistance movement.

43

Women of Prayer

In Amsterdam, where I lived with my mother and sisters and two girl cousins my age, the commander of the resistance had a secret office, from which he coordinated the various branches, initiatives, and groups of the underground movement, as we called ourselves.

My father died in the spring of 1944. One day during that summer, my older sister and I were asked to take part in this dangerous work as secretaries to the commander. Our burning desire was to bring liberation to our country and to see the end of the Jewish persecution. So we said yes to this proposition. No salaries were paid to resistance workers; we would only have been astonished if we had been offered money to do this work.

A few months later, I had to carry some papers to the resistance commander's private address as he was ill in bed. On that day I was stopped by the police. When they discovered those papers, I was arrested and put in prison.

The police went to my home and searched it but could not find anything which was forbidden or illegal. All the same, they arrested my mother, younger sister, and one cousin. My older sister and the other cousin escaped.

For safety reasons, neither my mother nor my younger sister had ever known what my work was. I also knew they would never say or do anything which might further endanger me. Not once, during or after the war, did any of my family members blame me for all the misery we went through. How good it is to be absolutely convinced about the loyalty of one's family.

Overcoming Fear in Prison

Day after day, I sat alone in my cell while fear gripped my heart. Would the German police question me again until deep in the night, as they had done that first evening? Would I be able to keep calm? Would there be torture?

Starvation? Fear lay like a brick at the pit of my stomach.

I knew only one way to battle fear and that was prayer. Every day I prayed until the fear left me. Sometimes it overwhelmed me again and I had to start praying once more.

The police threatened to hang me, my mother, and my sister (the persons I loved most on this earth), because they considered us to be spies. Then I was put into a dark cold cell with only water and very little bread. By keeping us deprived and in suspense, they hoped I would cooperate by answering their questions.

I was locked in a cell,
In a cell without light,
In a cell with a heavy bolt,
I shivered in the darkness,
So wintry, silent, and cold.

Arrested by German oppressors,
Who took my country by force,
I sat there in deathly silence,
Locked in by iron doors.

Only my steps on the concrete floor
Broke the silence and gloom;
Four steps to the left.
Four steps to the right.
Endless days without light.

How long would they leave me here
With only water and bread?
How could I battle this fear?
Torture seemed a real threat.
These men would force me to speak.

45

Women of Prayer

They had their methods, while I was weak.

Four steps to the left.
Four steps to the right.
How should I act,
How should I fight?

"Oh God, my Father, help me.
Do not let me perish here.
Take away my fear.
You are much higher than these men,
You are mighty, powerful.
Let their questions be in vain.
Don't let me weaken when in pain.
Oh Father, in your greatness,
You're my rock, my fortress."

Suddenly I stopped, amazed.
A picture came before my eyes.
It stretched far beyond my gaze.
It lost itself in space.
I stood there, stock-still, dazed.

The face of an enormous clock
Occupied the heavens.
So real and so wonderful
It gave me quite a shock.

There also was a pendulum,
Ridiculously small.
This pendulum could freely swing
But it could never fall.

I knew without a single doubt

The clock portrayed God Almighty,
And this little pendulum,
Only moving slightly,
Portrayed tiny me.
My insignificance
Was fastened to my God,
To His magnificence.

Enclosed in this somber gloom,
This hardship which I had to face,
Which spoke of death and doom,
God showed me my heav'nly place.
A place of great security,
For little pendulum-me.

Would I live or would I die?
It did not seem to matter.
He had answered my cry
With a vision, heavenly.
His greatness overwhelmed me.
His answer went beyond those bars.
Beyond this life, beyond the stars.
God's Majesty for ever.

God had given me an answer in a way no human being
is capable of doing. His answer went beyond death, for He
is God, God here on earth and God after death.

Although I was questioned once more, no one else was
arrested because of me.

But they put me back in that dark cell again—to stay
there for the duration, they said. Yet, very soon I was
taken back to the cell I had when I was first imprisoned.

I believe they had planned to send me to a concentration
camp in Germany, but the bombardments of the Dutch

railways by the allied forces made this impossible. The train which should have taken us to Germany had no tracks on which to travel.

We in the resistance stayed in prison, hoping, waiting, longing for the end of the war. We were kept in complete ignorance of world events, so it came as a beautiful surprise when we were freed on May 6th, 1945.

Free at Last

How marvelous was the sunshine and the flowers after months of stone walls and starvation. The Lord had brought us through. We were alive; we had survived.

Prayer made the difference.

Healing the Scars, Gaining Power

In 1976, I received the baptism in the Holy Spirit. During the seventies, I hardly thought of those months in prison back in 1944-45. It all seemed so long ago. But God knows our hearts better than we do ourselves, and the gentle Holy Spirit did something wonderful.

Once, after the baptism during my prayer time, the memory of the dark cell and all it represented came back to me. Then the soft voice of Jesus spoke very clearly to my heart:

"I was with you in that cell all the time."

Just those few words touched emotions I didn't know I still harbored in my heart, and I began to cry. Apparently there had been a scar on my soul without me knowing it. The tears brought relief and I experienced a certain release from a stress which I had not known was present in my subconscious. Jesus brought healing to my soul.

Translating Fear

About fifteen years ago, when Aglow had a few chapters

in Holland, I often drove our American speakers to the various Aglow groups. At the same time, I was their interpreter.

Although I spoke English fluently, I had never officially translated for anyone before. The first time I had to do this, I was pretty nervous. But when the Aglow board prayed with me beforehand, I felt much better; I knew they were there to encourage me, not to criticize every word I was going to say. Afterwards the president told me, "Your translation was all right, but you should smile more."

Still, I always felt nervous beforehand; I was afraid I might lose my concentration and then I would stand tongue-tied before a large group of women. A horrible thought!

"For the thing I greatly feared has come upon me, and what I dreaded has happened to me," says Job (Job 3:25), and so it happened to me. One day, I was busy translating when suddenly my concentration left me. I felt all my thoughts ebbing away, my brain seemed like sawdust, incapable of thinking coherently; it seemed to me I could not even hear the speaker properly anymore.

Asking for help was my only hope, so I silently called on Jesus. "Help Jesus, help!" And help He did: immediately my concentration came back, my thoughts were orderly again and I had no problem at all with what the speaker was saying. The right Dutch words flowed out of my mouth and nobody even noticed something had gone wrong.

It taught me how dependent I was on the Lord even in those things which I considered my own achievement. For that was how I had looked on my knowledge of the English language, "But," says Saint Paul, "our competence comes from God."

Jesus

He comforts me,
He strengthens me,
And tells me where to go.

He speaks to me
So tenderly,
It sets my heart AGLOW.

He teaches me,
He makes my spirit grow.

O Lord . . .
I love you so.

A Prayer of Obedience

In the summer of 1983 the Lord told me to leave the
National Board of Aglow Nederland. He did not give any
reason and at the time I did not understand it. After struggling with this change in plans, I said I would obey Him
and left the board.

Now I know that there was a difficult time ahead of me,
of which I knew nothing. But the Lord knows the future
and He knew I would need time, lots of time, to be
comforted by His love.

The heavy blow struck me in September 1985. One of
my daughters took her life after being under psychiatric
care for many years. I fell into deep mourning, crying,
wrestling with my emotions. It was a year in which I could
not do much work, and I certainly would not have wanted
to carry heavy responsibilities. I felt like someone who
needed to recuperate after a major operation.

The Lord is and was my . . .

Wonderful Counselor

I love to hear the voice of Jesus,
Guiding me and guarding me.
But this time I was angry,
For I thought He spoke unfairly.
Did I hear Him right?
I rebelled inside.

He said I was to stop this work,
Where, I thought, I could still grow.
Jesus' voice was very clear:
I should obey Him and let go.

I resisted three whole days,
But saw that I could never win.
Rebellion never pays
And so with many sighs,
I said I would give in.

Looking back on all those sighs
And on my lack of trust,
I see how wrong I was
And am ashamed of all the fuss.
How wise was His decision,
Timed with beautiful precision.

For sorrow, as a weeping cloud,
Wrapped itself 'round about
My soul, my thoughts, my brain.
Where was my human strength
In so much hurting pain?
I had to seek the Lord at length
For comfort, consolation.

51

Women of Prayer

> I needed time and privacy
> To shed my tears of desperation,
> Until He had strengthened me.
>
> He knew my need before it came.
> He gave me time to weep.
> How wonderful my Shepherd is,
> How well He leads His sheep.
>
> The breath of the Almighty
> Giveth understanding.
> The unfolding of His words
> Giveth light, unending.

How could I have come through that period without His comfort? Prayer made all the difference.

My Grumbling Prayer

More than a year before I was asked again to become a member of the National Board of Aglow Nederland, the Lord began speaking to me in my quiet time about a task He had for me.

When this had been going on for some time and nothing happened, I began to have doubts. I told the Lord I was already sixty-two, (as if He did not know), and that I was not getting any younger, (as if He had never thought of that). Also, I told Him how most of the women in Holland stop working between ages sixty and sixty-two, (as if the Lord needed this interesting information). And so I continued to grumble. . . . Couldn't He look for someone else to do the job? Someone younger?

I had to admit I was in good health, but I felt tired sometimes and often took a nap in the afternoon. Everybody always wants young people, dynamic people. Why me with my grey hair?

Grumble, grumble, grumble!

I did not expect an answer from the Lord; I know he does not like us grumbling, and so with a sigh one day, I turned to my daily Bible reading schedule. It said I had to start reading that day at Daniel, chapter six.

During my times with the Lord, sometimes I would read from the Living Bible and sometimes from my Dutch Bible. This morning I took my Dutch Bible and read the first verse:

"So Darius the Mede received the kingdom at about the age of sixty-two" (Dan. 5:31). I burst out laughing. The Lord had won the argument once and for all. All my grumbling disappeared as snow melting in the hot sun of the Lord's humor.

Just to be sure I also opened the English Bible and you know what? In the English translation this verse about Darius is the last verse of Daniel, chapter five. If I had accidentally read from the English Bible, I probably would not have seen this verse at all and would not have received this precise answer.

Even grumbling prayers make a difference.

New Life

On the day we meet the King
A change comes into everything.
Jesus is the Ruler—King;
In Him we trust, to Him we cling.

We feel His love and guidance;
Our horizon widens.
The cloak of praise descends on us;
God is holy, God is just.

A few years ago I spoke in one of our Aglow chapters about Naomi, who had lost her two sons. Even so, the Lord gave her a grandson to love, to take care of, and this grandson would continue the name of her son in Israel.

Afterwards, a lady came up to me for prayer. The Holy Spirit had deeply touched her heart during the message. She told me she and her husband had adopted two children because they could not have children of their own. This had been a great sorrow in her life, although she and her husband loved their adopted son and daughter, who grew up to be healthy young people. But it seemed as if her own sorrow was repeating itself. Her daughter had been married for ten years but had no children and also the four-year marriage of her son had stayed childless.

After the Aglow meeting, she was looking at her problem with new eyes.

When she came home, she wanted to tell the whole story to her husband, but she could not remember the names of Naomi and Ruth. So she went to look for a Bible in her home.

Years ago she had told herself that there was nothing in it for her. So the only Bible in the house was an old one inherited from her father. When she found the book of Ruth at last, she opened it to look for the names she could not remember. But God had planned this moment a long time ago.

To her utter amazement, the pages of the book of Ruth were all earmarked, undoubtedly earmarked by her praying father before he died. The Bible spoke to her in a surprising way. There were tears in her eyes. It seemed like a message from her earthly father to show her the love of her heavenly Father, who had been waiting for her all these years.

Some time later she came to my home for counseling.

Things of the past were put in order and old hurts healed by the gentle presence of Jesus. Before she left, we prayed together for her children.

A few months afterwards she called on the phone to tell me her daughter was pregnant. The grandmother-to-be was radiant. The Lord gives life and He gives abundantly. At the time of writing this chapter, her son also has a healthy baby and her daughter is expecting her second child.

> For with You is the fountain of life
> In Your light we see light (Ps. 36:9).

Prayer Makes a Difference

Prayer makes a difference in our whole life. It made a difference in my dark cell:

> Call upon Me in the day of trouble;
> I will deliver you, and you will glorify Me (Ps. 50:15).

Prayer made a difference even when I could only pray a very short prayer:

> I have called upon thee, for thou wilt hear me, O God
> (Ps. 17:6).

Prayer makes a difference, for then the Lord can tell us what we should do. He counsels and comforts us:

> The Lord is close to the brokenhearted
> And saves those who are crushed in spirit
> (Ps. 34:18 NIV).

Prayer makes a difference, even when we grumble, for He has a plan and purpose:

> Taste and see that the Lord is good (Ps. 34:8).

Women of Prayer

Prayer makes a difference for God is the source of life. Jesus says:

> I came that they might have life, and might have it abundantly (John 10:10 NAS).

Prayer makes a difference because God hears His children and answers them in His love and compassion.

> Because He has inclined His ear to me
> Therefore I shall call upon Him as long as I live
> (Ps. 16:2 NAS).

I love my Lord,
The living God,
Who answers when I call.

I love my Lord,
The living God,
The Father of us all.

QUIN SHERRER

Quin Sherrer, is the author of *How to Pray For Your Children*, Aglow's worldwide best-seller. She has co-authored three other books on prayer in recent years in an effort to give women tools with which to pray more effectively for their families and loved ones.

"Almost every day I get a letter from a hurting woman who has read one of my books, begging for ways to pray more effectively for her loved ones," she says.

Quin began writing for *Aglow* magazine in 1974 and has been an active Aglow leader for fifteen years. She served on the North West Florida Area Board for four years in the 1980s, after holding local offices in the Ft. Walton Beach, Florida, Aglow.

She was a U.S. board member from 1990-92 and presently serves on WAF's international board.

Quin has spoken on prayer in eight nations in the past four years, specifically on praying for families and using spiritual warfare on their behalf. She serves as an intercessor for several international Christian leaders and the Spiritual Warfare Network.

"To fulfill God's call on my life and those around me, I must be in His presence daily to get strategy for warfare, cleansing from sin, and hope for tomorrow."

4
. . .

How to Pray
For Our Families*

By Quin Sherrer

My tears spilled against the Wailing Wall in Jerusalem
that cool Sunday morning in February. Beside me was my
prayer partner, Laura, and on the men's side of the wall
my husband LeRoy was also interceding for our three
adult children, all wandering lambs.

Just a few days earlier when we walked through customs at the Tel Aviv airport, I spied a huge wall banner
showing Jewish people from all walks of life climbing up
the mountain to the temple in Jerusalem. The scripture
verse on the banner was a promise God had given me for
my children.

* Unless otherwise indicated, all Scripture references in this chapter are
from the New International Bible (NIV).

59

Women of Prayer

"'Restrain your voice from weeping and your eyes from tears, for your work will be rewarded,' declares the Lord. 'They will return from the land of the enemy. So there is hope for your future,' declares the LORD. 'Your children will return to their own land'" (Jer. 31:16-17).

Speaking Out the Promise

Now, leaning against the Wailing Wall, I reminded the Lord of it just as I had when I first saw that scripture banner. "Yes, my children will return from the land of the enemy. Thank you, Lord, that you will do it," I affirmed once again. "Even as the Jews are being drawn from all over the world to the nation of Israel, so my wandering children—mine and others like them—will return to the Lord," I said.

Leaving the Wailing Wall, we stopped to examine some olive wood handcarvings. I bought one of a shepherd lovingly carrying a lamb across his shoulders, just the way a shepherd brings back a stray lamb to the flock. My heart soared with hope.

For five years now we'd watched our children precariously walking in the land of the enemy. Though we'd raised them in a Christian home and in church, when they got to college they all tried the way of the world.

God Was Moving to Answer

A little later that Sunday night, God was about to miraculously answer one prayer more than 4,000 miles away from us.

Back in Florida, Sherry, our youngest, who was a senior at Florida State University, was preparing to drive the 125 miles from our home back to campus. A blinding rainstorm made her frightened to drive all that way alone.

Instead, she drove to town and circled three times around

the little church we attended, until at last the Holy Spirit
drew her inside. A visiting pastor from Africa spoke pas-
sionately on Matthew 6:33: "'But seek first his kingdom
and his righteousness, and all these things will be given to
you as well.'"

"God has a purpose for your life—and your job is to
find out what it is and do it," he insisted.

Sherry began to weep as the Holy Spirit stirred her
heart. "A purpose for my life . . . must I find out what it is
and do it, Lord?" Sherry questioned.

Steve Moore, a young man two years older than she,
approached Sherry and challenged her further:

"God is not putting up with you having one foot in the
world and one foot in the kingdom of God, Sherry. You better make up your mind, and you better make it up tonight."

Sherry continued to sob. And Jesus the Good Shepherd
found our lamb in Florida while we were still in Israel. I
later learned Steve had delayed his return to Bible school
because of the storm, allowing him to be in church at the
time Sherry was. His mom, a friend of mine, put Sherry in
their guest room overnight and got her up in time to drive
back to college classes Monday morning.

Forgiveness Is a Key

As soon as we got back from Israel, Sherry called to ask
us to come to Tallahassee and attend church with her.
After services, she almost dragged us to the altar with her.
Kneeling there she asked us to forgive her. We three wept
in each other's arms.

Assuring her of our forgiveness, I looked directly into
her eyes, "Sherry, there is no perfect parent and no perfect
child. Will you first forgive us for not being the parents we
should have been and for failing you so often?" She did,
she forgave us. And we all left the foot of the cross

cleansed and forgiven.

Our Sherry graduated from college then attended Christ for the Nations Bible school in Dallas where she met her Kim from Denmark. After their marriage and graduation, they moved to Copenhagen where they still live to do missions work.

God's Call on Our Children's Lives

Within eight months after Sherry's return to the Lord, our other two children, Quinett and Keith, recommitted their lives to Him. They, too, enrolled at Christ for the Nations and today continue to serve the Lord, using their artistic talents. Quinett makes worship banners that are used in almost a dozen countries. Keith is currently newsletter editor for Mercy Ships, an arm of the international Christian organization, Youth with a Mission or YWAM.

How grateful we were for the Lord's answer to our prayers for our three children after many difficult years.

What to Pray For

For years, I prayed for my children to have *godly friends, godly influences, and godly environment*. I also prayed for the *right friends* to come into their lives at the *right time*. In my prayer journal, I kept pictures of my children and names and photos of some of their friends whom, I knew, would influence them either positively or negatively.

While we are prone to pray for the wayward, we must not forget to pray for the godly ones who can help them walk the walk in their Christian path.

That's where Steve Moore came into the picture.

A Godly Man Whose Life Touched Many

Let me tell you about this godly young man, Steve. I'd prayed for him for at least eight years. On Fridays when I interceded for certain missionaries and pastors, Steve was included. I'd lay my hand on his picture and pray for him faithfully over those years while he served with Youth with a Mission's *Anastasis* mercy ship. I continued to pray when he later enrolled in Bible school, and when he wanted a Christian wife,—eight years of prayer—never knowing that God would use him on that rainy Florida night to challenge my Sherry in making a decision to fulfill God's purpose for her life.

Steve returned to Ft. Walton Beach, Florida, for his tenth class reunion and told as many of his former class-mates as he could about the Lord. Then without much sleep, he and his young wife drove toward North Carolina where a job was waiting for him as a youth pastor. Enroute, he hit a tree and met Jesus face to face—in heaven.

At age twenty-seven, Steve's life on earth ended.

Just before they closed his casket, I watched young men, all classmates of his, weep. "He told me about Jesus . . . just a few nights ago he told me about Jesus," one said.

The pastor gave an invitation at the funeral to anyone who would like to know Steve's Lord. At least six people raised their hands, including Steve's elderly grandfather.

Steve Moore, one whom the Lord had kept me praying for, was the human instrument God used to profoundly impact our family. Though I know Satan is the one who comes to kill, I somehow feel that Steve's purpose on earth was fulfilled in his short life span. God used him mightily. And as long as I have breath, I will not fail to tell his story.

A Covenant-Keeping God

My son, Keith, leaves this month for his third short visit to the mercy ship *Anastasis*. Currently, he's using his writing and graphic art skills to help communicate the message of this evangelical/medical relief arm of Youth With a Mission that sails literally around the world for Jesus.

Guess who helps support Keith and his new bride as they work for mercy ships: Steve Moore's parents! Steve, who had worked on his uncle's deep sea fishing boats as a very young boy, had been part of the first crew to repair this old ship to get it ready to sail as a Christian relief vessel offering medical care, relief aid, and hope to the desperate and needy.

God is a covenant-keeping God. He says he keeps "his covenant of love to a thousand generations of those who love him and keep his commandments." During our troubled years with our children, I often reminded Him of that promise in Deuteronomy 7:9.

Intercession Restricts the Enemy

Intercession restricts satanic forces and allows the Holy Spirit to bring *conviction, repentance, and godly change.* I see myself as standing between God and the person for whom I am praying, beseeching Him on their behalf; at the same time, I stand between Satan and that person, battling.

God's Design Includes Families

God is for families. The biblical patterns are promises for us today.

• When God told Noah to go into the ark, his entire family of eight was spared in the flood.

• When Rahab the harlot hid the spies in Jericho, she received protection from Joshua's invasion of her city—she and all her father's family.

• When Zacchaeus, a wealthy tax collector, faced Jesus, he agreed to repay all he had acquired through cheating. Jesus told him salvation had come to his house because "the Son of Man came to seek and to save what was lost" (Luke 19:10).

• Paul's jailer and all his family believed on the Lord Jesus and were saved.

• Cornelius, the first Gentile believer, accepted salvation when Peter preached in his home, and his relatives and close friends believed.

• Lydia was Paul's first European convert, and she and all her household were saved.

Salvation for households was God's design all along: For your family. For mine. Today Jesus Christ is the door to the ark (God's kingdom) for those who will accept Him. Our part is to pray our families into the ark.

I've kept a prayer journal for about eighteen years and can look back now and see what worked best for me.

No Formula

Let me warn you, there is no *formula* for prayer. Each of us must get into our prayer closets and get God's battle plan for specific situations in which we are interceding.

David and other great warriors we read about in the Old Testament inquired of the Lord before battle. Some experienced defeat when they didn't first ask God the warfare strategy.

I keep my Bible, notebook, and pen handy when I pray. The Bible gives me daily instructions. I call my prayer strategy the "Four W's": *worship* the Lord, then *wait* on Him to show me the *Word* God wants me to use in *warfare*. That doesn't mean that every day I'll do warfare, but I do know that Satan is the enemy, not my family members, so it is Satan's strongholds which we break in prayer.

Know Your Enemy

Scriptures that have helped me identify the enemy are

"Our struggle is not against flesh and blood, but against the rulers, against the authorities, against the powers of this dark world and against the spiritual forces of evil in the heavenly realms" (Eph. 6:12).

"Even if our gospel is veiled, it is veiled to those who are perishing. The god of this age has blinded the minds of unbelievers, so that they cannot see the light of the gospel of the glory of Christ." (2 Cor. 4:3-4).

Our authority, however, from Jesus, gives us power over the enemy. He has equipped us to take back the territory the enemy has stolen. Remembering that in His death and resurrection, Jesus conquered the devil, we enforce His authority as we battle His enemy. We keep in mind that Satan is only a fallen angel, not equal with God.

We Have Legal Right

Even though Satan has demonic evil spirits that carry out his assignments here on earth, as Christians, you and I have God's legal permission to forbid evil tormenting spirits and to loose their captives.

Jesus said, "I have given you authority to trample on snakes and scorpions and to overcome all the power of the enemy" (Luke 10:19).

Paul helped us see what our weapons are:

"I use God's mighty weapons, not those made by men, to knock down the devil's strongholds. These weapons can break down every proud argument against God and every wall that can be built to keep men from finding him. With these weapons I can capture rebels and bring them back to God, and change them into men whose hearts' desire is obedience to Christ" (2 Cor. 10:4, 5 TLB).

Targets and Strategies of Prayer

I often say, "Lord, help me *locate, identify, and pull*

down strongholds that are keeping my family members from your will. Give me targets of prayer."

A prayer pattern that had worked for me follows. But I caution you, find your best time to be alone with the Lord, to worship, and adore Him. And ask Him to teach you how to pray. Remember, there is no formula, except the one we call the Lord's Prayer and it is a powerful one to pray daily for your families.

Seven Prayer Strategies

• Pray the specific. Peter reminds us that it isn't God's will that any perish (2 Pet. 3:9), so I can quote His Word in my prayers.

• Pray the practical. As my son was about to graduate from Bible school, I prayed a practical prayer: for a *mate*, *money,* and *ministry* doors to open. When those were answered, I moved to other requests.

• Plant waiting prayers for the future. Pray for your family's future (even when you don't yet have grandchildren).

• Get a prayer partner or support team so you can pray with persistence on a regular basis. Two or more in agreement is a powerful weapon (see Matt. 18:19).

• Travail in prayer. Psalm 126:5 says those who sow in tears shall reap with joyful shouting. There will be times when you will have your own wailing wall in your quiet time with the Lord, interceding for those lost loved ones. But the day comes when we can shout with joy!

• Fast and pray. Dick Eastman says, "When you are about to take new territory from the enemy it is time to fast and pray. I call it fasting down the strongholds."[1] A holy fast will help loosen the bonds of wickedness and set the oppressed free (see Isaiah 58).

• Pray in tongues. Paul wrote the Romans that when we do, intercession keeps us by the Holy Spirit in the right strategic spot.

"The *name* of the Lord is a strong tower; the righteous run to it and are safe" (Prov. 18:10). We wield a powerful weapon with the words of our mouth, using the authority Jesus gave us—His name, His battle plan. I consider my greatest weapon is, when I speak, quoting God's Word aloud! I hear it, God hears it, and Satan and his evil forces hear it. It not only builds my faith, but helps route the enemy.

"Paga" (Paw-GAH) shouts the Israeli soldier when he hits the bull's-eye in target practice. Our intercession which has its roots in this Hebrew word, should hit the target in prayer.[2]

When Childen Wander

When my children were far from the Lord, there were two specific prayers I used against the enemy in my arsenal of prayer:

"The seed of the righteous will be delivered" (Prov. 11:21 KJV).

"All Thy children shall be taught of the Lord; and great shall be the peace of Thy children" (Isa. 54:13 KJV).

I'd say: "Satan, it is written, 'The seed of the righteous will be delivered.' I am righteous because of Jesus. My children are my seed and they will be delivered. All my children will be taught of the Lord and great will be my children's peace."

Then I'd thank the Lord that He would accomplish it.

"Let God arise and His enemy be scattered!" (Ps. 68:1) I'd shout.

My two *warfare* prayers are found in Acts 26:18 and in Second Timothy 2:25-26; I used these scriptures as I called out names of family members who had turned their backs on the Lord. Look these up and apply them when they fit your set of circumstances in praying for lost family members. Remember that godly ones need prayer, also: I often prayed portions of chapter one and two from the book of Daniel for my children when they were students.

Prayer Tactics

Once when one of our son's high school friends gave him advice contrary to what we'd taught him, I was led to pray as David did about Absalom, that the advice he was getting would be as *foolishness*. Keith told me shortly afterwards that he realized how foolish the things the boy had told him were—just as I'd prayed.

However, the next time we recognized a wrong influence through one of Keith's acquaintances, we prayed differently. "The Lord turned the captivity of Job when he prayed for his friends," my husband and I read one night (Job 42:10 KJV). In agreement, we decided to pray much for the boy who was having a bad influence on Keith. "Lord, your Kingdom come, your will be done in _____'s life," we prayed often. No longer did we beg the Lord to remove him; we prayed for God's purpose to be accomplished.

But imagine our happiness when very shortly afterwards he received a four-year college scholarship that moved him far away from our son. God truly blessed Keith.

Defend Your Field

"I view my family as my 'bean patch' to defend through prayer," Jamie Buckingham, writing in *The Nazarene,* said. "The responsibility of being good managers of God's vineyard has now passed to us. Each of us has a sacred obligation, to take care of the field where we are placed, to protect it from the enemy, to see the harvest is taken, and to give back to the owner his rightful share. . . .

"Keep watch over your field, your vineyard: your family . . . all the things you are responsible for. You are the tenant manager. But Never forget who owns the field."[3]

There's a story in the Old Testament about one of David's three mighty men named Shammah with whom I've been identifying lately by recognizing my responsibility to defend my "bean patch" in spiritual warfare. Shammah means *Jehovah is present.* Here's his story:

When the Philistines banded together at a place where there was a field full of lentils, Israel's troops fled from them. But Shammah took his stand in the middle of the field. He defended it and struck the Philistines down, and the Lord brought about a great victory (2 Samuel 23:11-12).

Notice that everyone fled but Shammah. He took his stand in the field—his territory—and defended it. And the Lord, who is ever present, brought the victory, striking down the enemy.

Keep Watch on the Wall

God is calling us as watchmen on the wall who can learn during prayer *how* and *what* God wants accomplished through prayer. Nehemiah told the Jewish remnant rebuilding the broken down walls in Jerusalem:

"Remember the Lord who is great and awesome, and fight for your brothers, your sons, your daughters, your wives, and your houses" (Neh 4:14 NAS).

JOAN MORTON

"It is a fact that the word of God will always play a major part in any individual's prayer life." So says Joan Morton, national president of Women's Aglow Fellowship, Australia, for thirteen years.

Since she helped found Aglow in Australia sixteen years ago, Joan has borne a vision for women in her country that has caught fire in all six territories across the continent "down under," as well as Tasmania, and planted 112 local Aglow fellowships. She is a sought-after speaker throughout Australia and southeast Asian nations.

Operating from an office in Sydney, Joan has helped organize Aglow prayer and evangelism "trekking" missions to those on farms and sheep stations who are separated from each other by hours of surface travel.

She considers three key parts of her personal prayer life: "Seeking God for my own life and the work He has called me to; praying with my husband, which enriches my life and brings a togetherness; and wearing the breastplate of righteousness as I have written about in this chapter."

5
...

How to Pray as Busy Women
(A Prayer Closet in Our Hearts)

By Joan Morton

God has laid His hand on many people whose major involvement in their Christian living is spending several hours in prayer and intercession. I honor them in their calling.

My words in this chapter, however, are for those whom God has called to "wear many hats" during the day—busy women, particularly leaders—for whom hours spent in prayer does not seem possible on a daily basis.

Yet, we must be in communion with God for the sake of others, which is a part of every committed Christian's life, busy or not. The question becomes, how do we do it when God has called some of us to be wives, mothers, and active in ministry at the same time?

My Need to Find an Answer

It was the need and cry of my own heart to find how to do my part in prayer within my calling. And it was not my heart's cry alone.

I have found that wherever I minister, busy women hunger to be part of God's plan in the world by praying, and yet they are unable to spend those hours before God's throne and remain faithful to their responsibilities as mothers and wives, business, community, church, or outreach leaders.

The Pain of Condemnation

Let me share one example. Recently, I received a phone call from a local Aglow president who was distraught that she could not spend two or three hours in prayer each day. As we talked, she listed her other responsibilities: She worked part-time, had three children, a very busy husband, and a small activity in her local church, as well as her Aglow position.

If a busy woman such as this Aglow president does not find a way to have communion and relationship with God, it brings about a self-condemnation in her spirit that is worse than what brought her to this spiritual crisis—her lack of being able to spend hours in prayer. She feels that she doesn't pray long enough to be actively involved in ministry or to have an effective relationship with the Lord.

Whether that condemnation comes from others or herself, often it results in the woman deciding that she should resign most or all of her activities (thus giving the enemy another victory), whereas that is not always the answer.

When I realized there were thousands out there who were experiencing the same crisis wrought by the necessarily busy life of a woman, I was desperate for God to give me an answer. I sought God and was so comforted in the response that the Holy Spirit gave me, I want to share with you that comfort from His Word.

Praying in Jesus' Name

The first point I wish to address is the scripture in Revelation 19:13: "He is dressed in a robe dyed by dipping in blood, and the title by which He is called is The Word of God" (TAB). I am well aware that there is a doctrine in which many do not agree, called praying in Jesus' name. I refer to this scripture when I say the following: We do not use those words as a cliché or a signing off of our prayer. I want to express that when we pray in Jesus' name, we are actually praying in the whole Word of God. We are simply affirming and confirming that it is Jesus in whom we trust, in His name, we are praying.

Praying without Spoken Words

My next point is that the scripture in Romans 8:26-27 says that the Holy Spirit prays through us with groanings that cannot be uttered or even with tears. Indeed, when the Spirit prays through us, we are truly praying in the will of God.

I wonder if you have ever thought that in giving the Holy Spirit His rightful place in your life and acknowledging that you are the temple of the Holy Spirit, that which you have assumed must be said out loud, can be borne in your spirit, your body, and your mind without a word being spoken.

It is certainly something we need to appreciate, because we have been of the understanding in Christian culture that our praying is expressed mostly with words.

I want you to know that I am genuinely experiencing the creativity of the Holy Spirit in this regard: I can bear grief, I can be groaning on the inside for a particular person or circumstance, I can be weeping without people seeing tears. To me, this way is going to be a very new and special area many of us will enter and develop.

Situations for Silence

I read a book that blessed me some years ago entitled *Of Whom the World is not Worthy*, about praying without words. What intrigued me was that the families who were portrayed prayed very much from the closet of their hearts because they could not pray any other way. They were in prison camps.

When they escaped from prison camp during World War II, they were in hiding and danger almost every day.

The author was telling us that the Holy Spirit is a creative facilitator of the will and the heart of God. Because He is also the One who indwells us, who brings out the cry of our own hearts and melds it with the heart of God, somehow He reaches out of our spirit into the heavenlies where God dwells. Then whatever is in us—crying or groaning or weeping—is a prayer to the Father prayed from the closet of the heart.

The Function of Our Mind

When the heavenly Father created us, He gave us a specific area called our mind. It can certainly be used to our detriment or to our good.

Two scriptures are very significant here and can be prayed from the closet of our heart through our mind. They can be effectual fervent prayers that God will hear without our speaking a word. One is in Hosea 14:2, "Come to Me with your words . . . His ear is never heavy that He cannot hear." The second is from Philippians 1:28. "Do not [for a moment] be frightened or intimidated in anything by your opponent and adversaries, for such [constancy and fearlessness] will be a clear sign, (proof and seal) to them of [their impending] destruction; but [a sure token and evidence] of your deliverance and salvation, and that from God" (TAB).

How wonderful to be able to use the faculties of our mind connected to our hearts in union with the scriptures that have been written on our hearts, that we might not sin against God. When we want to cry out from the closet of our hearts to God through our minds, the scriptures that we have learned can be offered as prayer to the Father no matter what situation, what place, or what circumstance we find ourselves in.

Our Permanent Breastplate for Priesthood

The Holy Spirit led me next to Exodus 28. This chapter contains a vivid description of the garments that God said were to be made for those who were to be in the priesthood. In verse three it says, "Tell all who are expert, whom I have endowed with good skill and good judgment that they shall make Aaron's garments to sanctify him for my priesthood" (TAB).

Please note that these garments were preparing him for the priesthood; those words also speak of our relationship with God and our communion with Him.

The specific part of the priestly garments I want us to look at is the breastplate. Exodus 28:15 tells us, "You shall make a breastplate of judgment in skilled work; like the workmanship of the ephod, shall you make it, of gold, blue, purple and scarlet stuff, and of fine twined linen" (TAB). Set in this breastplate were four rows of three stones in each row and on those stones were engraved the names of the sons of Israel. The high priest wore this breastplate.

Also on his shoulders were the skillfully woven girding straps that had a stone on each shoulder with six names on each stone. God's creativity is magnificent!

Let me share some thoughts concerning the breastplate. The thrill of what God showed me is very real and very vivid in my spirit and in my heart as I write. (I trust you will take your Bible at some point in time and read this chapter in Exodus through and through to realize how significant a part the garments played in the priest's life, particularly the breastplate.)

> They shall bind the breastplate by its rings to the rings of the ephod with a lace of blue, that it may be above the skillfully woven girding band of the ephod that the breastplate may not come loose from the ephod.
>
> So Aaron shall bear the names of the sons of Israel in the breastplate of judgment upon his heart when he goes into the holy place, to bring them into continual remembrance before the Lord. In the breastplate of judgment you shall put the Urim and the Thummim [unspecified articles used when the high priest asked God's counsel for all Israel]; they shall be upon Aaron's heart when he goes in before the Lord, and Aaron shall bear the judgment, (rights and judicial decisions) of the Israelites upon his heart before the Lord continually (Ex. 28:28-30 TAB).

Closet of the Heart

The closet of the heart is the deepest area the Holy Spirit can penetrate to place God's desires and our desires in order to be prayed through. Now we know all Scripture is given for our inspiration and we are very much aware that Jesus is our great High Priest. But we are also aware that He made us to be kings and priests to Himself. I believe the breastplate is an answer to praying effectively as busy women, in the prayer closet of our hearts.

In using the breastplate as an analogy, I realize that I, as a priest to God, can wear a breastplate—that part of the priest's garments that sanctified him to the Lord. And as I wear that breastplate, which has twelve stones on it, I remember the twelve names written there.

As the Holy Spirit opened this truth to me, I saw that as I let God know my spirit was open to Him to speak to me, He could give me names of more people that I could wear daily on my breastplate and have on my heart all day and even all night, names that were involved in many, many situations and circumstances.

Remember, the breastplate of the high priest was placed so that it could not move; the priest brought it continually before the Lord every time he entered the Lord's presence.

I found as I put on, as it were, my breastplate, the Holy Spirit would daily quicken to me names to be inscribed on the stones. Some were placed there for a length of time, but as I knew in my spirit that the Holy Spirit had prayed through these names, He would give me another name, and other circumstances to pray for.

As each day dawned in the closet of my heart, I was conscious that in my daily time with Him, *however long or short*, He would continue to give me names that I would place on those stones of my breastplate. As I went to work, to ministry, or to the market, I knew that those names were on the breastplate and in my spirit; they were continually before the Lord. What a precious place the closet of the heart is. What a sacred place it is!

Now I do this daily and will continue with this practice always.

There is another side to wearing the breastplate with the names on the stones. It is not just the beauty and magnificence of the work of the Holy Spirit when you are praying. I began to see something deeper in the closet of my heart: Many answers to prayer came, many lives were affected, and yet no one knew. There were no words spoken out where they would be public knowledge. It was between God, the Holy Spirit, and myself.

The wearing of the breastplate is a way of praying in the closet of your heart which is truly in obscurity. Yet I want to assure you that it is very effective; it is a pure work of prayer and the Lord gets all the glory.

As we examine our real role when we put on our breastplate, it is exactly the high priest's role.

Our Take-Along Prayer Closet

Many times as I sat in a car or on a bus, a grief would enter my heart for one of those names on the stones. I found myself reaching out to God in my spirit for circumstances in the life of someone named on the stone at that particular time. Luke 19:41 says as Jesus drew near, He saw the city and wept over it. How I knew that experience as I saw in my spirit people, churches, circumstances because their names were written on my breastplate.

My spirit also prays in every other way that it ever prayed, when I am kneeling or sitting before my God, verbalizing the cry and desire of my heart in prayer.

Condemnation Lifted

At one particular seminar when I ministered this subject of wearing the breastplate, several women came up afterward and told me that condemnation had been lifted from their lives with regard to the amount of time they spent in the Lord's presence.

I also had an Aglow area president tell me that before hearing this Word from the Lord, she felt she should resign because she could not spend two or three hours a day in prayer. She worked alongside her husband in the field on their property, almost from daylight to dark. Now she said, "I can now be praying all the time and be more effective than I have ever been because I struggled and wept in self-condemnation, trying to pray in the little time I had."

God wants prayer to become a victorious way of life in our spirits twenty-four hours a day, not a struggling and striving. As we take hold of the power that God is alive in us by the Holy Spirit, we develop the expectation and anticipation of that prayer life within us as we wear our breastplate.

I pray that the Spirit will quicken to you busy women that there is a place in the closet of your heart where you can pray continually and that you will develop this attitude of prayer.

Then in those precious times when you are able to draw aside for a longer time to be with God, they will be richer and fuller because you have already been dwelling in the richness and the awesomeness of the God you love and serve. This, I believe, meets the desire of your heart to be a part of the praying Body of Christ, which will usher in His kingdom.

Live with Expectation

A word which comes into my heart constantly these days is that somewhere we can lack expectation in what we know of and want from God. If we have no expectation in us, it will never happen. God wants our prayer life to become a continual way of life: we can expect the Holy Spirit to come to us with thoughts and impressions. We will be quickened to pray right where we are, in the closet of our heart.

Women of Prayer

I expect God to place on my heart daily, all that I have expressed with regard to the breastplate. I expect the Holy Spirit to quicken me to pray for whoever and whatever. It can be across the other side of the world or here in my own city. It all has to do with my heart attitude to prayer and the expectation that God knows my heart and that my spirit is alive with His Holy Spirit. I am His vessel who wants to be involved in whatever He desires to place upon me.

With all the changes that are taking place around us, let us make a quality decision to express to God that our expectations are of Him. Hope will continually be in our hearts as a result and from that hope will come faith, and from faith leading to faith, as Hebrews says, will come the prayer from the closet of the heart.

Perhaps if you say daily, "Holy Spirit, I am expecting you to speak into my being today the desires of the Father's heart," the results of your decision will develop from expectation to great anticipation and excitement day-by-day as to what the Holy Spirit will bring forth.

Lesson in Silence

I would like to include this story from Australia. Several years ago God placed a desire on my heart to go to Ayers Rock, the world's largest monolith, which lies in the geographical center of our nation. If you do not know anything about Ayers Rock, a map of Australia will show you how very large it is, rising 348 metres (over 1,000 feet) high over the desert floor, and eight kilometres (over seven U.S. miles) in circumference. This giant red stone, visible for miles around, lies a few hours' drive southwest of the town of Alice Springs, located in the Northern Territories.

Ayers Rock is not only at the heart of our nation, it is known by us as the heart of the darkness of our nation.

With a desire in my heart to pierce the darkness, I planned a seven-day prayer journey with twenty-two women from all over Australia. Once we gathered together in this district, we spent the morning waiting on God and asking for keys, asking the Holy Spirit for strategies. Then we traveled to the rock by bus in the afternoon.

During that whole week, the strategy the Lord gave us was continually one of silence, prayer going up to the heavenlies from our hearts alone.

We went out to that rock every day and marched around it silently. Our spirits, our hearts, our minds, our whole beings were filled with the anticipation and expectation that the cries which were in our very being, in the deepest part of the closet of our heart, were going up to the Father for the stronghold of darkness to be broken over our nation.

Because of the great darkness, one would think we had to use every other method in spiritual warfare. But God continued to give us the word, *silence*, and *be silent*.

We came home from that prayer journey knowing that much was accomplished in the heavenlies for our nation.

Powerful Prayers from the Heart

Remember in 1 Samuel 1:13 when Hannah was distressed and prayed before the Lord: "Now Hannah spoke in her heart; only her lips moved, but her voice was not heard"? Hannah's prayer before God was very powerful and resulted in the desire of her heart.

In Oswald Chambers' classic devotional book, *My Utmost for His Highest*, he says, "He, the Spirit in you, maketh intercession according to the will of God. God searches your heart not to know what your conscious prayers are, but to find out what is the prayer of the Holy Spirit." Chambers goes on to make this magnificent statement: "The Spirit of God needs the nature of the believer as a shrine in which to offer His intercession."[2] How more could our spirit be the shrine of His intercession, as we, whose bodies are the temples of the Holy Spirit, wear the breastplate daily with the names on those stones?

Praying Above and Beyond Circumstance

It is not just the busyness of our lives, but our changing circumstances that will necessitate the need. It will be a method of survival in this day and age, survival so that there is a heart/spirit response which reaches out to God through our mind, in order that we do not react to circumstances and conditions that could be thrown upon us at any moment.

I simply want to convey thoughts that will bless and provoke you in all your busyness, that you can be very much a part of God's praying people.

For closet prayer to be developed in its fullest is to bring about what the Lord is wanting to do in our own cities first, our own nations, and the world.

May your spirit and your nature be responsive to the Spirit of God.

Section II

Called to the Nations

The Spirit of Prayer

CINDY JACOBS

Cindy Jacobs, an ordained minister, is often called a spiritual warfare specialist. As president of Generals of Intercession, a ministry that prays for the United States and other nations in the world, Cindy speaks to a broad range of the Body of Christ. She serves on the Aglow International Board as well as on the Aglow International Prayer Council.

Cindy has traveled to many nations to meet and counsel with prayer leaders who have a heart to tear down satanic strongholds over their cities, states, and nations. She has ministered in Argentina to church and lay leaders involved in that country's revival.

"I try to spend two hours of prayer with the Lord each day that I'm not on the road," she says. "One of the keys to prayer I practice is taking time to listen to the Lord. Prayer is a two-way street. Sometimes we are so busy talking, we can't hear God's answer."

Cindy's vision is to see the majority of Aglow women in regular intercessory prayer meetings in order that thousands of women in the nations of the world will find Jesus Christ as their personal Savior.

6

. . .

Dethroning Reigning Strongholds

By Cindy Jacobs

A magnificent banquet was prepared by the king. Invitations were sent across the nations requesting the presence of the powers of Persia and Media, the nobles, and the princes from over 127 provinces from India to Ethiopia.

The nations were called to a feast at which the king showed the riches of his glorious kingdom and the splendor of his excellent majesty for 180 days. When these days were completed, the king gave a banquet that lasted seven days in the court of the palace garden. It was for the people, great and small, who were present in Shushan, the citadel garden of the king's palace.

For this grand occasion the king employed his best interior decorators to dress the garden. The curtains were white and blue linen, fastened with cords of fine linen and purple on silver rods and marble pillars. The couches were of gold and silver. Guests sat on a mosaic pavement of alabaster, turquoise, and white and black marble.

Not only was the setting lavish and extravagant, the drinks were served in one-of-a-kind golden goblets. Each man could drink or not drink according to his own wishes.

At the end of the seven days the king was very merry with wine. As he looked around at the assembled male guests, he began to think about what a sensation his beautiful wife would cause, wearing her royal crown into the banquet hall for all the men to see.

Her name was Vashti and she was giving a banquet for the women in her apartment within the palace. When the king's eunuchs came with his command to join him, she refused to go.

Why didn't Queen Vashti come when the king called her?

Could it be that she did not come because it was not traditional for her to do so? Perhaps she was shy or too proud to come.

We *do* know that the king commanded her to leave her own banquet and for whatever reason, she refused. Because the king's advisors feared that Vashti's behavior would "become known to all women, so that they will despise their husbands . . ." (Es. 1:17), she was dethroned by the king and another queen chosen.

Our Invitation from the King

The Spirit of God is moving powerfully across the nations today, issuing us invitations to come into the court of the King. Unlike Queen Vashti, we know that whenever our King calls, he has our best interests at heart.

In this world-wide move of intercessory prayer, God is

entreating us, "It's time to pray! Ask Me for the nations, cry out to Me for the salvation of your family, your city, your country."

Even though many of us are hearing the call to prayer, many others struggle with coming into the court of the King, in order to intercede. If God is for us, what stands between us and the destiny He has for us in prayer both individually and corporately?

Strongholds Reign

Many times it is called strongholds. Strongholds are fortified places Satan builds to exalt himself against the knowledge and plans of God.[1] These strongholds can effectively paralyze us and keep us from answering the call of God, from entering the throne room when our King bids us, come.

I am sure that many reading this have been challenged by Mordecai's words, "Yet who knows whether you have come to the kingdom for such a time as this?" (Esther 4:14) This challenge elicited a powerful response from the new Queen Esther, "Call the nation to fasting and prayer. If I perish, I perish!" (Esther 4:16).

Women of God, it's time to receive the calling of Esther. We will dethrone strongholds that reign in our lives when we are willing to face them, to deal with them, and to make a vow to God that *nothing* will stand in the way of our following Christ. God wants to use His women as a mighty army to stand up, look around our communities and say to Satan, "Enough is enough! You will not pollute the minds of our children with humanism, defile their minds and bodies with pornography, and abort unborn children." We can move these mountains when we become Esthers for our nations.

God is asking women to pick up the scepter of the King

and come close to His throne. This is an end time move of the Holy Spirit. There is a wonderful prophetic promise given by Peter in Acts 2:17-18 (when he quotes Joel).

And it shall come to pass in the last days, says God, that I will pour out of My Spirit on all flesh. . . . on My menservants and on *My maidservants* I will pour our My Spirit in those days.

In this chapter, I want to share what I know about five major strongholds and then give you some keys to break their power.

1. Strongholds of the Mind

One of the primary strongholds that keeps us out of the throne room of prayer is what I call strongholds of the mind. I like the definition Edgardo Silvoso, president of Harvest Evangelism in Argentina, gives this type of stronghold: "A mind-set impregnated with hopelessness that causes the believer to accept as unchangeable something that he/she knows is contrary to the will of God."[2] In other words, there are ways we think and feel about ourselves and situations in our lives that are contrary to God's will.

The Bible says nothing is impossible with God. However, because of different circumstances, mind-sets form and scream out the opposite message to us. These mind-sets tear at us with negative thoughts such as, "Stop praying for your husband's salvation. He'll never be born-again." or, "God can't use you. Look at the terrible things you've done in your life." Satan plays on these thoughts because he knows that prayer really works and wants to stop us from praying at all cost!

2. Strongholds of Fear

One of the biggest strongholds we women struggle with is fear. Fear comes in many packages and hides behind lies. We sometimes self-righteously dress up fear as, "It's simply not *me* to stand in public and pray." I can write about this stronghold of fear because it has been a big one in my life.

Years ago I lived with fear, especially fear of people. This strangled me from praying in public. My tongue would glue itself to the roof of my mouth when it was my turn to pray. (I guess it's a testimony to the delivering power of God that people often laugh in disbelief when I tell them, because I often pray quite forcefully now).

The church I attended when Mike my husband and I were first married had a Wednesday night prayer meeting; we would come together and take turns praying out loud. Each week I would rehearse in my mind what I was going to pray and how I was going to say it and, alas, each week would go by without my uttering a sound! One day I came upon the scripture in Proverbs 29:25: "The fear of man brings a snare, but whosoever trusts in the Lord shall be safe."

This scripture gave me courage and I vowed to God I would pray the next week. Wednesday seemed to come around very quickly. On my way to church, I kept thinking about my vow to God. That night I had a tremendous breakthrough! I didn't pray a long prayer but I did pray out loud. What a victory! Each time after that, I would work on it some more until the stronghold of the fear of people was uprooted in my life.

Fear of Others' Opinions

Another way the fear of other people controls women is through fear of their opinions: What will people say if I stand up for the things of Christ publicly? What if I attend meetings to pray against pornography or the drug problem in our schools? What if the Lord should not only want me to pray but to speak up when I see things that aren't pleasing to Him in my child's school, in the city, or grocery store?

One day I was in our local discount store when I saw a magazine with an extremely explicit picture of a woman on the front cover. I had a choice. I could close my eyes and pretend not to see it and tell myself I was too busy to do something, or I could live my prayers. I gathered the magazine from the stand and asked to see the manager.

When he arrived I quietly said to him, "Sir, I am the mother of a young boy and I don't want him to come into your store and see this kind of picture displayed." Immediately, the manager went over to the magazine rack and removed all copies of that particular magazine. Victory! The old Cindy, bound by the stronghold of fear, would have passed that opportunity by.

There are many kinds of fear and it seems I had to tackle them one by one. A deep-seated problem in my life was the fear of inadequacy. Sometimes such a fear stems from physical problems beyond our seeming control. Many great women of the Christian faith have grappled with this problem.

One such woman was Catherine Booth.

"Few women of any generation have been as influential in the Kingdom as Catherine Booth, 'Mother of the Salvation Army,'" writes biographer Charles Ludwig. "Yet her immense influence can only be understood when viewed against the backdrop of the adversity and impossibilities she faced. Suffering from a severe spinal disease when only fourteen, her formal education came to an abrupt end. At eighteen, she was confined to bed for six months with tuberculosis. As the wife of William Booth, she raised eight children despite her frail condition."[3]

Catherine was a prayer warrior and learned to win her battles over inadequacy in the prayer closet, refusing to let them stop her from serving Christ.

There are many modern day women just like Catherine Booth. One is Jane Hansen, president of Aglow, a woman who has overcome strongholds of fear. Jane shares her story in her autobiography, *Inside a Woman*. It is a story of courage, faith, love, and prayer. Jane is not a natural extrovert. In fact, one part of her life that she did not share in her book was how God took her from being a secretary at Aglow headquarters to becoming international president.

God called Jane to a destiny in Christ that would require her to overthrow her natural reticence about being in the limelight. Jane had a choice when the call came and she said, "yes," not because she felt adequate or prepared, but because she had come to the same place Esther had when God wanted to use her to save a nation.

Esther also must have struggled with the call of God. Susan Goodnight writes about Esther in chapter one of this book: "She was, after all, a prisoner of war, a child without parents, one certainly not born into position. Her sudden change of life, power and prestige must have been overwhelming."[4]

Some might have thought Esther was from the wrong ethnic group to be queen. Not only that, when we read about the terrible things that happened to her in her formative years, we can see that she came from a dysfunctional background, as well. There were most likely real obstacles in Esther's life. Yet, despite her own inadequacy, Esther rose up to the call of God on her life. She prayed, she fasted, and then she entered the throne room and took the scepter offered by the king.

I believe we need healing from life's hurts. But

sometimes we use them as excuses not to progress. The pain of yesterday engulfs us until we refuse to try again. But we can never fully be all we are meant to be until we are willing to yield ourselves to God's destiny for our lives. We must press toward the mark for the high calling (Phil. 3:14). We must press on to get whole and rid ourselves of the strongholds that tie us down. God is always ready to do a work in us.

3. Strongholds of Intimidation

Intimidation often binds women. It occurs when we look at our shortfalls rather than at the greatness of God. It seems that when we are in a prayer meeting and asked to share those praise reports that are part of the complete cycle of intercession, the devil sends a hoard of demons to sit on our shoulder and shout, "Who do you think you are? What right do you have to share? Everyone will think you are full of pride if you tell how God answered your prayer." Of course, Satan's motive is to keep God from being glorified.

He uses the same methods when we try to sing for the Lord or testify in any way. It's simply the same song, second verse. If we are hearing these things, we are probably the very ones who should be singing or testifying. You know those times in a prayer meeting when it becomes really quiet and the leader says, "I feel someone needs to share something from the Lord." One way you can tell it is you, is that your heart starts pounding, your mouth suddenly becomes completely dry, and fear hits your body like a Dallas Cowboys' linebacker.

A key scripture in overcoming the strongman of fear and/or intimidation in our lives is found in 2 Timothy 1:7. I like the way the Amplified version reads:

For God did not give us a spirit of timidity—of cowardice, of craven and cringing and fawning fear—but [He has given us a spirit] of power and of love and of calm and well-balanced mind and discipline and self-control.

4. Generational Strongholds

Some strongholds start long before a person is born. You might say, "Wait a minute, Cindy, that's not fair!" True, certainly, true. I have never—not ever—found the devil to play fair. There is an enlightening scripture in Exodus 20:5:

For I, the Lord your God, am a jealous God, visiting the iniquity of the fathers on the children to the third and fourth generations of those who hate Me.

This scripture essentially means there are particular types of sin your parents have yielded to that causes you to reap the effects of as their children. It doesn't mean, however, that if the parents commit murder, the children are murderers before God. But it does mean that the family can be susceptible to the same kind of sin their parents committed. Because of God's law of visiting iniquity to the third and fourth generations, strongholds or weaknesses in character and nature are frequently produced in the seed of people who commit the sin.

Let me give you an example: If a pregnant women has excessive x-rays, the child she is carrying may be deformed through being exposed to the rays. Now it isn't the child's fault; the child is a victim. Nevertheless, he is still deformed. This is the way iniquities are passed through the generations. Sin is the cause, and iniquity is the effect in the same way the x-rays were the cause and deformity the effect.

Women of Prayer

We could say that the sin of the fathers is an open door through which Satan can strike us when we move to a place of prayer. It is a hole in our armor. We need to close those holes by repenting of the generational sins of our family. Many people move out in intercessory prayer only to get hit with infirmities or financial problems. Deuteronomy 28 gives an interesting list of curses that come upon families as a result of sin. Among them are insanity, poverty, and infirmity.

The Bible is full of people who were affected by the sins of their fathers and fell into the same types of sins, only in worse ways. Quin Sherrer and Ruthanne Garlock talk about this type of stronghold in detail, in their excellent book, *A Woman's Guide to Spiritual Warfare*: "Look at Abraham, the patriarch we laud as a godly example. On two occasions he lied about his wife, Sarah, calling her his sister. Then Abraham's son, Isaac, lied about his wife, Rebekah, saying she was his sister. Isaac's son, Jacob, deceived him so he could receive the blessing due the firstborn, Esau. Jacob's older sons deceived him about his younger son, Joseph, causing him to grieve for years. The tendency to lie and deceive showed up in succeeding generations, each time causing more serious consequences."[5]

Maybe you're thinking right now, I thought we were free from the curse of the law. Absolutely right! Galatians 3:13 boldly states: "Christ has redeemed us from the curse of the law, having become a curse for us."

Let me ask you a question in return. Are you automatically born again? Are you automatically healed? No, you have to ask for these things. It is the same for obtaining freedom from generational sin. We need to ask forgiveness for the sins of our forefathers just as Nehemiah and Daniel did.

What happens when we ask forgiveness for the things

our parents and those who came before us did? Of course, they are still responsible for their sin before God, but Satan loses the legal right of entrance to accuse us before God for these sins. We have shut the door on the devil. I have seen many people healed as a result of confessing sins their parents committed, such as love of money, idolatry, worship of ancestors, or vows made to secret societies such as freemasonry.

In addition, many people have experienced a tremendous release in their finances after repenting for the sins of their fathers in certain areas, such as the sin of robbing God through not tithing. People who regularly tithe, but are still not experiencing the blessing of God, may need to repent in this area.

5. Strongholds of Tradition

One of the deepest strongholds in my life, one that prevented me for years from becoming a prayer leader, was tradition. As I've already pointed out, this very well could have been one reason Vashti refused to come to the king during his "men only" banquet. Sometimes strongholds within our culture or even religious systems can bind us from fulfilling our full calling and election in serving God.

Please permit me to explain by telling you a little of my story about how I dethroned the old monarch of southern culture in my life.

I was a nine-year-old at a church camp in Prescott, Arizona, when the counselor advised, "Go find a place to talk to God alone and ask Him what He wants you to do with your life." I hiked to a big rock in the woods. As I sat on that rock, the Lord called me to give my whole life to Him for full-time Christian service.

Later at the evening meeting, an invitation was given and I began to weep. I'll never forget the song that was sung, "I Surrender All." That night with all my heart, I did just that. When I went forward, I was asked to fill out a form. I knew I couldn't be a pastor because only men could do that so I checked the space that said "missionary."

Years passed and nothing seemed to happen. Little did I know that it would be twenty-one years before I understood what God was asking of me.

I graduated from college and became a music teacher. I got married and had two children.

When I turned thirty I remember thinking, "Lord, now will You tell me why You called me on that rock in the woods?" It seemed as if the heavens were like brass and the only thing I thought I was hearing was, "Wait." Wait? What had I been doing for twenty-one years?

All of a sudden I had a brilliant idea. I would pray for God to call my husband Mike into full-time Christian service. You know the prayer: Here am I, Lord . . . send my husband!

It fit in with my southern culture and with the teaching of the denomination I had grown up in. Everything was perfect about it, right?

Wrong.

God had a different idea. One I didn't like very much.

That year our family moved to Weatherford, Texas, and before I turned thirty-one, a restlessness came over me. I kept reading a scripture that troubled me.

He who loves father or mother more than Me is not worthy of Me. And he who loves *son* or *daughter* more than Me is not worthy of Me. And he who does not take up his cross and follow Me is not worthy of Me. He who finds his life will lose it, and he who loses his life for My sake will find it (Matt. 10:37-39).

Was God trying to tell me He wasn't going to negotiate about sending me instead of Mike? What would people think? Why me, a woman? What about all those scriptures about women not teaching? I had a suspicion that whatever the Lord wanted me to do involved traveling. Nice southern ladies do not leave their homes. I told you earlier that we have a son and a daughter, Daniel and Mary. I wasn't going to lay my children down on any altar of ministry. No way!

Furthermore, I had been a preacher's child and I knew what children go through when their parents are in the ministry. What would mine have to face with their mother— a woman—in the ministry?

Why Me, Lord?

On one particularly difficult night I was crying out to God, "Lord, there are many men you could use, why do you need me?" I was sitting with my Bible on my lap and I opened it to read. My eyes fell on the scripture that says, "Woe to him who strives with his Maker! . . . Shall the clay say to him who forms it, 'What are you making?' " (Isa. 45:9). Quietly in my heart the Lord said, "Cindy, stop fighting against the way I have made you. I want you not only to say yes, but to like how I've made you. I want you to embrace the call of God. I have called you to be a maidservant of the most high God. If I am going to pour My spirit out on *all* flesh in the end times, (Joel 2:28-29), then some people I choose have to be women!"

Even after that, I found myself walking the floor, night after night, weeping, wrestling with God. Finally one night the Lord spoke to me, "Cindy, give Me Daniel and Mary. I want you to take up your cross and follow Me." I answered, "Lord, can't I give them to You when they are older? I would be of much more use to You when I am

101

fifty and they are grown up." Again the still small voice, "Cindy, give Me your children." I began to weep as I made the trek up the Mt. Moriah in my heart to lay Daniel and Mary before the Lord as Abraham had laid Isaac.

A beautiful thing happened after that; deep peace settled into my soul. The peace of surrendering all. I knew what God wanted because Psalm 2:8 was coming to me over and over again: "Ask of Me, and I will give You the nations for Your inheritance, and the ends of the earth for Your possession." The call of God on my life was a call to the nations.

Funny thing, though. At first, my husband Mike wasn't really thrilled. "Who's going to wash my clothes, cook my dinner and clean the house if you are called to the nations?" he asked.

Good question.

Not only was God asking a lot of me, He was asking for a great deal of sacrifice on Mike's part. It was then that I found I had to surrender the call of God back to the Lord as God began to work in Mike.

A Year of Preparation

During the next year, I fasted and prayed for my family. This was a preparation time of purification such as Esther went through. It was a time of learning to intercede. It was a time of deep cleansing. During this year, God spoke to Mike from Scripture about women in the ministry. As time went on, Mike began to bring me scriptures he had discovered in the Bible. Mike was the first to show me: "There is neither Jew nor Greek, there is neither slave nor free, *there is neither male nor female*, for you are all one in Christ Jesus" (Gal. 3:28).

This verse was important because it made Mike realize that ministry is not a gender issue, but an anointing issue.

I also found books that explained scriptures regarding

102

women, such as the *Magna Carta for Women* by Jessie Penn Lewis. Other excellent books also deal this subject: *Who Says a Woman Can't Teach* by Charles Trombley, and *I Suffer Not a Woman* by Richard and Catherine Clark Droeger.

As I prayed for my family as my first ministry, God brought us into agreement that since there is no male or female in Christ, a woman could lead prayer in mixed groups as well as preach the Gospel.

Doors Opened

Doors for ministry started to open quickly for me. It was almost scary how rapidly things began to move. It's funny how God seems to move so slowly that it takes forever, and then He speeds up so fast it takes your breath away to keep up!

What We Need to Ask Ourselves

What stops us from serving the Lord in prayer?

Sometimes it may be a matter of time. When one has small children, it may be difficult to have long periods of time alone. Mothers of small children sometimes have fulfilling prayer partnerships by phone during nap time. It is also possible with today's phone systems to arrange a conference call to pray as a three-fold cord prayer meeting. I have found with my busy life, I have to put the name of Jesus on my schedule just like I would any other appointment, to make sure I have time with Him alone in intercessory prayer.

Breaking Strongholds

Here are a few keys to breaking strongholds in your life:

1. Identify the strongholds one by one. Rather than working on everything at once, take one and begin to zero in on that area.

2. Make a commitment before the Lord to be whole in that area of your life.

3. Ask the Lord to show you any root causes (e.g. woundedess, wrong thinking, generational strongholds, pride) that would hold you back from serving in the court of the King.

4. If you have believed a lie about yourself (for instance, you are too shy to ever pray aloud in a prayer meeting), confess this to the Lord and vow to change.

5. Seek the Lord for the areas of intercessory prayer He wants you to cover. Is there a particular nation that has really been on your heart? What issues in your community need to be touched through prayer? Some women, for instance, pray together for their children's schools.

6. Join a prayer group and/or ask the Lord to give you a prayer partner.

7. Study current materials on intercessory prayer and find out what tools are available to assist you in training as an intercessor. Aglow has a powerful prayer map for fellowship members. Every Home for Christ has a world prayer map to help you pray around the world each day. The book, *Operation World* by Patrick Johnstone is a powerful tool to help you pray for the nations of the world.

Dethroning Prayer

What kinds of reigning strongholds do we still have in our lives? Whatever motivated Vashti, it cost her the crown, her rightful title, her position. But her king was human, subject to pride and anger and condemnation.

Our King wants nothing but the best for us, He wants us to complete our destiny in Him.

If you realize you have some strongholds in your life that need dethroning, pray this prayer with me:

Father, I want to dethrone those things in my life that have kept me from serving You as an Esther. Lord, I now enthrone You as Lord in their place in my life. Today, I surrender all to You and will serve You as You have called me. I accept my position as an intercessor for the King of kings. In Jesus' name. Amen.

You are off on one of the greatest and most exciting adventures of your life. Truly you have come to the Kingdom *for such a time as this* to pray for your family, city, and nation and see them won for Christ!

CHRISTIANA BOATEMAA DARKO

In 1992 Christiana Boatemaa Darko and her husband were faced with a life-changing decision. Her husband's possible candidacy for the presidency of the nation of Ghana, Africa, sent her to wait on the Lord in fasting and prayer for three days to discern God's will for their lives.

Kawabena Darko lost the election in a very close race, but the Christian witness that he and Christiana presented to their nation will long be remembered.

Christiana both began and became president of the first affiliated Aglow fellowship in Ghana, which met at her home in Kumasi in 1985. After eight years, Aglow Ghana now has forty-three affiliated groups. Currently, she serves on Aglow's International Board as International Outreach Director. "We encourage Aglow women in West Africa to be the Esthers of our day," she says. "Aglow women are to stand in the gap and pray for Africa."

Christiana has been active in church activities since her youth, but was not born again until 1965 when another student nurse witnessed to her.

The Darkos have six children including an adopted daughter.

7
...

Waiting on the Lord

By Christiana Boatemaa Darko

Those who wait upon the Lord shall renew their strength. They shall mount up with wings like eagles. They shall run and not be weary, they shall walk and not faint (Isa. 40:31).

We live in a quick-fix environment. The billboards read: instant coffee, instant cure, instant this and that. We find them appealing because most of us like it when things happen immediately.

We never enjoy waiting. We are impatient and get upset if everything doesn't come to pass the way we plan. In my case, I find it difficult to wait while I am expecting my children to return home after long visits away.

Allow me to give you another example from my own life: In 1991 after the Aglow international convention in Orlando, Florida, USA, I visited a medical doctor at Antigua, an island in the Caribbean, for nutritional treatment for gall bladder stones.

I looked forward to seeing some results on the first day, but nothing happened. On the second day, I became impatient and wondered if the medication was really worthwhile. A few nights later while I was sleeping, the Lord spoke to me in a song:

Be still my soul; the Lord is on your side.
Wait patiently the cross of grief or pain.
Leave to thy God to provide.
In every change He faithfully will remain.
Be still my soul; thy best, thy heavenly
Friend through thorny ways leads to a joyful end.

I got up quickly and started thanking the Lord. A few hours later when I visited the bathroom, lo and behold, stones came out of me. Since then, I have been praying for a waiting spirit, because an impatient spirit is not of God.

An impatient spirit means you are running ahead of God, and in the end you suffer. Often, impatience turns to anger.

I experienced such anger one night when my husband didn't arrive home from a business trip by midnight. He travels a great deal and prefers to drive home even at a late hour to sleep in his own bed. That night my impatience caused me to grumble about his being out so late. Finally I went to sleep. The door bell woke me up, and I was so annoyed I did not welcome him home after such a long, hard trip. My angry, impatient attitude destroyed any warmth between us that night. I have since repented of those actions.

Our Patient Role Models in the Bible

The Bible has many examples of people who had to wait for a long time, sometimes many years, to receive their breakthroughs.

The children of Israel called on Jehovah God to send them a deliverer. That took about 400 years of praying.

• Moses, the deliverer, had to wait for forty years in the land of Midian till God spoke to him to deliver the children of Israel. I am sure there were times when Moses asked himself if he was really in the will of God. Let us not forget his circumstances: He was out there on the back side of the desert with only the sheep for company.

• Jacob loved Rachel and prayed to God to give her to him in marriage. It was not a quick-fix situation. He waited for fourteen years to have his prayer answered, and it involved frustrations and plain treachery.

• Hannah prayed to God for a child. It took year after year of waiting upon God to receive her answer. But praise the Lord, the answer came.

• Anna the prophetess waited upon God day and night for many years. She was an old woman before she saw the Messiah Jesus Christ coming into the temple in Mary's arms.

• David recognized that he could not do anything without divine guidance. Therefore he prayed to God to lead him into the truth and also to teach him to receive from the Lord. In order to do that, he had to exercise patience by waiting on God for His final instructions, a patience that would be needed for his leadership role ahead.

Our Greatest Example

Jesus is our greatest example of waiting on the Lord. The Gospels of Mark and Luke give us a picture of the

111

waiting periods of our Master:

"Now in the morning, having risen a long while before daylight He went out and departed to a solitary place; and there He prayed" (Mark 1:35).

"And when He had sent them away, He departed to the mountain to pray" (Mark 6:46).

"Then the report went around concerning Him all the more; and great multitudes came together to hear, and to be healed by Him of their infirmities. So He Himself often withdrew into the wilderness and prayed" (Luke 5:15-16).

"Now it came to pass in those days, that He went out to the mountain to pray, and continued all night in prayer to God" (Luke 6:12).

"And He was withdrawn from them about a stone's throw, and He knelt down and prayed, saying, Father, if it is Your will, remove this cup from Me; nevertheless not My will but Yours be done" (Luke 22:41-42).

From these times of solitude, Jesus returned with renewed strength, and a new anointing that enabled Him to heal and deliver the afflicted.

Waiting for God's Wisdom

As leaders or committed members of Aglow, we need to wait on God's wisdom to be able to lead the people God has entrusted into our care. Solomon asked nothing from the Lord but wisdom. God knows what is best for our lives because wisdom is one of His attributes. James says, "If any of you lacks wisdom, let him ask of God who gives to all men liberally and without reproach and it will be given to him" (Jas. 1:5). We get into trouble when we go our own way, by trying to trust in ourselves. In 1 Corinthians Paul writes, "For the wisdom of this world is foolishness with God" (3:19).

112

God's wisdom proved vital to my success in 1971 when I was elected women's ministries president of our local church. I was twenty-seven years old—too young to lead the older women who, at that time, ranged in age from forty to sixty years. In Africa, an older woman will not take the counsel of someone young enough to be her daughter. It takes a woman of the same age to advise her.

I realized I could not successfully fulfill this office at my age by my own strength. I needed wisdom to speak with them and wisdom to guide them into the truth. I started praying for God to give me His own wisdom to be able to lead these mothers. (Note: In our African culture, it is a sign of respect to address a mature woman as "Mother"). At our meetings, we averaged about forty women every Friday morning.

The Lord honored my prayer and gave me His wisdom as I waited on Him, more than I asked for. Previously, the young women in the church never attended the women's ministry meetings; now they were challenged to join, knowing that they had a young woman as leader.

Even though the Lord heard my prayer for wisdom, gaining the trust of these older women was a process, not without some mistakes. I remember one meeting when respect for elders was burned into my mind. I was sharing the Word of God about why it is necessary not to be yoked with unbelievers by drinking liquor during funerals and other cultural rituals. One older woman who had been regularly involved with such rituals stood up in front of everyone and shouted, "You are my daughter, how dare you judge me!"

Immediately, I knelt before all the women and asked her forgiveness for offending her. I realized then that at every meeting, I needed to wait on God for an understanding heart, a humble and obedient spirit, a wider vision, and the ability to open my mouth with wisdom.

God gives us wisdom to enable us to do the things He wants us to do. It is not acquired quickly. It is bestowed upon hearts and minds that have learned to wait upon Him.

Waiting for Anointing

God will anoint us and fill us with His power if we will wait on Him in prayer and fasting. In ourselves we are weak and helpless, but through His power we are filled with His anointing to see things done in His name. We need that anointing if we are going to reach the world for Jesus.

In ministering to women, we need the fullness of the anointing to release conviction, healing, and deliverance. It is the anointing that destroys the yoke.

Often, there is a need to wait on God for a specified number of days in preparation for the full anointing. At our Aglow bi-monthly, one-day retreats, we fast and pray. Before outreach breakfast meetings, some Aglow fellowships organize three-day fasting and prayer times in preparation. Waiting on the Lord has always brought special anointing, often with healings.

When we held Ghana's first national Aglow convention in 1988, I prayed and fasted for days, before and during the convention. We saw an extraordinary anointing throughout the conference with healings and deliverances. Many fell under the power of the Holy Spirit during worship.

Jesus said, "The Spirit of the Lord is upon Me, because He has anointed Me to preach the gospel to the poor. He has sent Me to lead the brokenhearted, to preach deliverance to the captives and recovery of sight to the blind. to set at liberty them who are oppressed" (Luke 4:18).

Jesus had to wait upon God in the wilderness forty days and forty nights without food and drink for that anointing.

David was anointed by Samuel to be king over Israel when he was a youth, but David waited fifteen years before he finally became king. First Samuel 16:13 declares, "The Spirit of the Lord was upon David from that day forward."

Waiting for the Word of the Lord

Waiting on God's instruction has also helped me in my ministry. In Psalm 32:8, God says, "I will instruct you and teach you in the way you should go; I will guide you with My eye."

When the Lord Jesus was sent to the wilderness by the Holy Spirit after His baptism by John, He waited for God's instruction from His Word as well as for God's anointing. The Word became alive in His spirit. He wielded the Word of God with great boldness and defeated Satan with the sword of the Spirit.

As we wait on the Lord, we need to study the Scriptures to guide us. We are admonished in Psalm 119:105, "Your word is a lamp to my feet and a light to my path." The Word of God should be desired by all who wait on Him.

In 1992 the Lord spoke to my heart while I was waiting on Him in prayer. He reminded me again of the scripture in 2 Timothy 2:15, "Study to show thyself approved unto God, a workman that needeth not to be ashamed, rightly dividing the word of truth" (KJV).

This scripture was what sent me, as a young woman, to the Christian Service College, an interdenominational Bible college at Kwadaso, Kumasi in Ghana. Three years later, I received my diploma in Bible studies and another diploma in theology from the University of Ghana, Legon.

Waiting on God's instruction then was not easy. I had already studied hard to be a nurse, but as I studied the Bible and waited patiently those three years in Christian Service College, God taught me things I needed to know.

He is the greatest teacher of all and has taught me to divide the word of truth confidently by His power.

Waiting for Timing

Finally, let us wait on God for His timing. "To everything there is a season, a time for every purpose under heaven" (Eccles. 3:1). God has time for everything; He is never too early or too late.

Many a time, we complain about delays in getting our prayers answered. Sometimes God says yes instantly, sometimes He says wait.

As a director of our family poultry business, Darko Farms & Co., I have learned that it always takes twenty-one days for a chicken to hatch from the egg. We cannot speed up the process; otherwise we will have a stillborn chick.

Timing For Marriage

Many single women have been waiting on the Lord for their life partners. In the African culture, unmarried women are not respected in society; thus marriage is a priority for every Christian woman. When a woman marries, she enters into a new life of womanhood. She has dignity, honor, and respect. At the core is the traditional African view of womanhood: she is made for fertility, to fetch water, prepare food, and look after the home.

Unmarried women and barren married women still suffer a social stigma in Africa because of the importance placed on fertility. The woman is blamed if there are no children in a marriage and is scorned by other women because of the African concept of ideal womanhood. No wonder Christian single women feel discouraged as they grow older, yet their prayers for a marriage partner remain unanswered.

Some become so impatient that they marry any man who comes their way, whether he is a Christian or not. In the process they find themselves living in a relationship that is contrary to the word of God.

God's Promise While We Wait for Him

Sisters, we can never change God's timing. We just have to wait on Him. God has a beautiful plan for each one of us, but He tests and tries us in order to develop patience and perseverance. The limitless rewards of His power and grace are worth it.

PAULA SHIELDS

Twenty-five years ago, Paula Shields attended the first Aglow meeting in Seattle, Washington, and has been an integral part of the ministry ever since.

As Aglow's Outreach Director for Western Europe for the past eight years, Paula spends much time in God's presence before she "puts feet to prayer" in traveling through the nations.

She has participated in Aglow leadership since 1968, initially as president of the first local Aglow fellowship in the world in Edmonds, Washington; later, she became international Bible study chairwoman. From 1976-1982, Paula served as vice-president for leadership training and concentrated on foreign fellowships in 1982.

Paula shares a singularly profound experience from her prayer life: "When others talked about feeling the Father's love, I so desired this, too. But I had never experienced many 'feelings' when I prayed.

"Someone told me that feeling came by faith, so I prayed, 'Father, I am coming into your presence by faith. The way has been accomplished through the blood of Jesus.' As I prayed to be in my Father's presence, a beautiful peace enveloped me—I experienced a deep sense of security . . . no words were needed . . . I felt loved! I had known this through the Word of God but this was a completion of it."

8

. . .

Healing Prayer*

By Paula Shields

When He, the Spirit of truth, comes, He will guide you into all the truth [and] He will teach you all things (John 16:13, 14:26).

When I pray for healing, whether emotional or physical, I know that only God, through the power of His Holy Spirit, can perform this healing. It is only as we empty ourselves of self and allow God to fill us with His power, truth, and grace, that the lives of others can be touched, healed, and saved.

In Scripture, we are promised that we carry the Holy

---

* Unless otherwise indicated, all Scripture references in this chapter are from the New American Standard Bible (NAS).

Women of Prayer

Spirit in us (1 Cor. 3:16); that He helps us to know how to pray for others (Rom. 8:26); that He will bring comfort, be the Counselor and the intercessor (John 14:16-17); that when we pray for others, the gifts of the Holy Spirit are available to us (1 Cor. 12:8-10).

Our prayers for someone to be healed appropriates all that Jesus has already accomplished for us. He bore our sickness and grief and carried our sorrows. He was wounded for our transgressions and crushed for our iniquities (Isa. 53:4). Today Jesus is with us and in us to bring His healing love to those who have been wounded by rejection, disappointments, sorrows, and other griefs in their lives.

European Experience

When I first went to Europe, I was appalled at how much time it took through an interpreter just to learn about a person's problems and pain. After awhile I began to ask the Holy Spirit to show me the root of the problem and how to pray. I discovered that He is always faithful.

Since then as I pray for physical healing, emotional healing, or deliverance, I have learned to be completely dependent upon the Holy Spirit.

As I have stepped out in faith and trust in the Holy Spirit to guide my prayers, I have become more and more aware of His desire to bring healing to people and to set them free. Over and over I have experienced His faithfulness to do so. As I pray for a person, I see the gifts of the Holy Spirit all working together—a word of knowledge or prophecy is frequently accompanied by the distinguishing of spirits, the release of the gifts of healing, and the growth of faith.

I want to share some of these healing experiences with you. Because emotional healing was the kind I needed most, God has used me primarily in this area of healing.

Forgiveness and Judgment

I have read that eighty percent of our walk as Christians is receiving and accepting forgiveness. Just as we have received forgiveness, we in turn must forgive. We have no choice. But that forgiveness must come from the heart. Many times when there is forgiveness from the mouth, but not the heart, we remain tormented. The prayer of forgiveness is a key to being set free from the enemy and brings a deep healing.

At an Aglow retreat where I was speaking, the counselors brought a young woman to me whom no one had been able to help. Her head was down, and she wouldn't look at me. I asked her, "What is your need for prayer?"

"I have committed the unpardonable sin," she answered in a flat voice.

When I asked her, "What is this sin?" she finally told me that she had had two abortions. I responded, "I also have had two abortions and have accepted Jesus' forgiveness." I then told her that Jesus wanted to forgive her, too. I shared with her that in order to be set free I had confessed full responsibility for the decision to have the abortions and had confessed that I had murdered my two children—that when she did this, she, too, could receive forgiveness.

I prayed with her to receive God's forgiveness and to be set free from all condemnation and guilt. As she prayed and received forgiveness, she quietly started to speak in tongues. She had desired this gift for two years, but guilt and condemnation had kept her from being released in the Holy Spirit. The next day few people recognized her as she came to breakfast with a glowing smile on her face, now a beautiful woman changed by the prayer of asking for and receiving forgiveness.

123

Through this experience, I learned that God will cause all things to work together for good to make us more like Jesus (Rom. 8:28). As I am vulnerable and open in the areas of my life where I have been healed, the person I am praying for receives faith to believe that she too can be healed.

In Matthew, Jesus taught, "Do not judge lest you be judged; . . . By your standard of measure, it will be measured to you" (7:2).

I believe that this scripture means that whatever judgments we put on someone else will come back on us. We attach ourselves to whatever we have not forgiven.

When we become believers, even though we ask for forgiveness and forgive others, deep inside our hearts we often are still resentful and judgmental of those who have hurt us. In my own life I discovered roots of bitterness that started in my childhood with resentful judgments against my parents.

The Holy Spirit made me aware of judgments I had held against my mother as a child. The things I was holding against her were not really truths, but how I as a child perceived them. When the Holy Spirit showed me this through a dream, I immediately asked Jesus to forgive me for holding these judgments in my heart. I prayed to Him to loose them and so to free my mother and myself.

I was healed not only in my heart, but also from an infirmity. For a number of years, I had continually suffered from constipation. With this prayer of forgiveness, I was healed and have never again had this problem.

We all see sins and weaknesses passed down from one generation to another (Num. 14:18). If we will go back into our childhood at specific ages and times, asking Jesus for His grace (help) to forgive, He will faithfully enable us to forgive. When we follow this by asking forgiveness for our judging and to stop this bitterness from being passed from one generation to another, He will do it.

Sexual Abuse

Sexual abuse is running rampant in our society. But as I pray for sexually abused women and men I find that many times I am the first person with whom they have shared what happened to them.

One young woman came to me because she was having a terrible problem with lust. In fact, her lustful desires had caused her divorce. As we prayed together, she shared how she had been sexually abused by her sister's boy-friend when she was eleven.

Because of this abuse, she felt guilty and unclean. In addition, it had opened the door to lust and perversion. When I told her that Jesus could come and minister to the child who had been abused, she asked. "How can Jesus be there? It was so . . . bad (sinful)." But as I prayed for her in the Spirit, she suddenly sensed a great peace. She experienced Jesus' power and love releasing her from her false guilt and cleansing her body from all that had happened.

The words of love the Lord spoke to her closed the doors through which the enemy could return as she accepted Jesus' forgiveness for herself and forgave the young man. Although I had additional times of prayer with her, this was the beginning of her healing.

Incest, in particular, is tremendously damaging to a person's relationship with our heavenly Father. It causes a great fear, and the person who is assaulted builds up walls of self-protection within herself that keep Jesus out.

Another woman I prayed with had been sexually abused by her father. As I prayed with this woman, I repeated over and over again, "You were a child, a victim." I did this to break the lie which so many sexually abused people carry around with them—the lie that says they are responsible for what happened. We asked Jesus to come to her, but when she couldn't sense His presence, I told her, "You need to forgive your father as Jesus has forgiven you." She insisted she couldn't do this, but I reassured her, "That's right, you can't, but we'll ask Jesus to give you the grace to forgive." Then when she asked Jesus to help her, the grace did come, and the bitterness and anger were released. As she, the child, forgave her father and released him from judgment, she experienced Jesus' presence, along with His peace and love. She also felt a cleansing of her body and mind, and for the first time experienced being in her heavenly Father's presence.

I prayed for another young woman who was the victim of incest at the hands of her father and brother. She hated her body and said over and over, "I cannot forgive." I continued to encourage her to ask Jesus to help her. I prayed with her to remember the first time the abuse had happened with her father. Then with Jesus helping, she released forgiveness to her father and set him free from her judgment. We prayed the same release for her brother, and again Jesus' presence was there to help as we prayed. Next I prayed for the cleansing of her body and mind by the blood of Jesus. Although I knew by the changed expression on her face that this prayer had brought some healing, I didn't realize to what extent until I saw her later. That night at the worship time, she danced up to the front of the auditorium—her body free to praise God. Here was this woman who had said, "I hate my body," dancing beautifully before the Lord. Truly a prayer of healing had set her free!

Healing the Broken Hearted

I pray for people with broken hearts in a slightly different way. Often I start with scripture. I quote Psalm 34:18,

"The Lord is near to the brokenhearted and saves those who are crushed in spirit"; Psalm 147:3, "He heals the brokenhearted and binds up their wounds"; or Isaiah 61:1-3, "The Spirit of the Sovereign Lord is on me, because the Lord has anointed me to preach good news to the poor. He has sent me to bind up the brokenhearted, to proclaim freedom for the captives and release from darkness for the prisoners, to proclaim the year of the Lord's favor and the day of vengeance of our God, to comfort all who mourn, and provide for those who grieve in Zion—to bestow on them a crown of beauty instead of ashes, the oil of gladness instead of mourning, and a garment of praise instead of a spirit of despair" (NIV).

As we pray, I tell people to picture Jesus by faith, standing or sitting beside them. When they see Him, I tell them, "Now ask Jesus to show you your heart, the hurt, the pain, and to bring those feelings to the surface so that they can be healed." We name these pains—the pain of rejection, the pain of disappointment, the pain of sorrow. Next I tell them, "Now just put your heart into Jesus' hands, and as Jesus takes it, let it go and let your pain go with it—let all the hurt go."

As Jesus takes their hearts, I tell them to see themselves at whatever age they were when their heart was broken. I might pray a prayer similar to this: "Lord, let them see You as the God of all comfort, who comforts us in all our distresses. Let them feel Your love around them, let them feel You hold them in that love. God, let them feel Your comfort, Your unconditional love, the security of Your love. Oh, Father, give them the love they need. Now, Father, remove the pain and the hurt. Make their hearts completely whole. Lord, where they've built a protective wall around their hearts, pull it away very gently."

As I pray for them, I visualize Jesus taking their heart

and I see Him healing it and making it completely whole. If the Lord shows me anything to say, I say it, and if He doesn't, I don't. I pray until I get a release that it's been accomplished.

Here, as in all healing, I want people to see and experience Jesus' presence. It is only Jesus who heals. I encourage them to visualize Him loving them. If the heartbreak occurred during childhood, I might say, "Just see Jesus loving you. See Him picking you up and holding you in His arms." I find wherever I go, there are people with broken hearts. As only Jesus can heal them, this is a vital prayer ministry.

Healing from Injuries Suffered in the Mother's Womb

It is now an accepted medical fact that unborn children can hear voices and they can also recognize those voices after they're born. Unfortunately, an unborn child can also pick up the mother's emotions—feelings of loving and wanting the child or feelings of rejection and fear.

A child carries these feelings into her childhood and even though she may later receive love, she can still be tormented by overwhelming feelings of rejection.

I was healed of this kind of rejection years ago. Before my mother became pregnant with me, she had planned to leave my father because of his unfaithfulness, but the pregnancy prevented her from doing so. Consequently I wasn't a "wanted" child, and my mother's feelings were transmitted to me in the womb. Although my mother loved me after I was born, I remember how hurt I was whenever my parents teasingly called me "their little mistake." As I grew up, I never truly felt loved by them.

At a large meeting I attended, the main speaker had finished his message and was praying a healing prayer over the whole group. As he prayed for an unborn child who felt rejected and not wanted, I started to cry, and deep inside me I felt a warmth of love touching a coldness I had carried deep within me my whole life.

As the speaker prayed, Jesus' healing love took away the feeling of rejection and replaced it with His warmth and peace, and I knew at that time Jesus had touched me with His healing love.

Since then I have prayed for many for this same healing—simply asking Jesus' love to heal and take away their rejection and fear and release forgiveness to the parents.

The Word of Knowledge

There was a young man in a church where I was speaking who had been repeatedly violent as people prayed for him. They said they had prayed deliverance for him many times, but he continued to have the same problem.

They brought him to me, with a person on each side of him, holding him in case he became violent. I laid my hand on him and immediately I saw a picture of his father beating him, a little boy of ten. It was a vicious, angry beating. I said, "Your father beat you when you were young." "Yes," he admitted with some amazement, "but how did you know?"

I told him that God had given me the information by the gift of knowledge and that God knew everything about what had happened to him as a child, that God loved him and wanted to set him free from the pain and bitterness.

"Let's have that little ten-year-old boy forgive his father for beating and punishing him without any reason. You were innocent and suffered injustice."

As I prayed, he asked Jesus to help him forgive his father for hurting him and to set him free from his judgment and resentment. Tears flowed down his cheeks. His expression changed to one of peace as he experienced

Women of Prayer

Jesus' presence and the healing of that injured little boy, now set free from his bitterness.

Karin, my co-worker, and I were praying for a man who asked for prayer concerning his bad relationship with his father. Because of it he was having a difficult time having a loving, trusting relationship with his heavenly Father.

As we prayed for him in the spirit, Karin had a word of knowledge that he was feeling pain around his neck. He acknowledged that he felt as though he were choking. The Holy Spirit then brought back a memory of when he was quite young and his father had picked him up by the neck. The little boy within him forgave his father, the pain in his neck left, and he was set free to trust and love God.

The Prophetic Word

The prophetic word, which comes from God to bring edification, exaltation, and comfort (1 Cor. 14:3), has the power to heal when spoken into a life.

I was praying for a pastor who had been depressed and discouraged for a long time. He had been in a serious automobile accident, and miraculously his life had been saved. He knew God had spared his life for a purpose, but many things had happened to cause disappointment in his ministry, in people, and in himself. He was frustrated and angry.

I prayed with him in the spirit. I knew he needed a prayer from the heart of God. As I continued to pray for a few minutes, the word from God came: "The past is gone. As you have been saved in this accident you are born again—the past is gone, and I will make all things new. You don't need to be mature. You are free to be a baby—to be born again." With this word, all his self-judgments were broken.

I saw that he received the word with joy and that he truly felt the presence of the Lord. But I didn't realize how much this prayer had accomplished till I saw him a few weeks later. His eyes were sparkling as he greeted me. "Paula, I'm changed—really born again. I now read and enjoy the Bible like I haven't for a long time. I pray and fast, which I haven't for a long time. I love people I didn't like before. I can't believe what has happened. I am truly born again."

A prayer to change—a prophetic word to set free!

It is easy for daughters to judge their mothers. We love them and we want them to be perfect. But so often as we see our mothers' imperfections, we say, "I won't be like that. I won't do that when I grow up." Yet unfortunately we find ourselves bound to that which we have judged.

I prayed with a woman who had this problem. She thought of herself as a very weak woman, saying, "I can't do this." "I can't do that." As I prayed for her, the Lord showed me that she was really a strong woman but was afraid of being strong. I told her this, and she cried and said, "Yes, I don't want to be like my mother."

As she spoke out, I could see that the judgment against her mother needed to be broken. She cried like a child and said, "I don't want to be like her—strong and controlling." I prayed with her and she forgave her mother for controlling her. She also asked forgiveness for having judged her.

As she set her mother free from her judgment, she also was set free. We prayed that she would be set free from the control she had experienced from her mother and from her mother's influence. In prayer, I placed her under the influence of her heavenly Father, to be like Him, to be free, to be the woman God has purposed her to be. She could be strong, but under His Lordship and influence. As I prayed, the Holy Spirit gave me these words of God, "Perfect love (Jesus) casts out fear and torment." I prayed that Jesus' perfect love would cast out all her fear.

131

I could see as the tense expression left her face that she was now set free from these fears. Now she could be self-reliant and capable and not fear being controlling and domineering.

As I pray for women around the world, I have found out how faithful the Holy Spirit is to provide all that is needed. Jesus came for those who need healing—healing is His ministry, and His desire is to set His people free.

SHARON BARRETT

Sharon Barrett, director of U.S. Fellowships, believes "God is calling Aglow and all women in a special way never witnessed in the earth before this generation. He is releasing them to become an integral part of all He is doing in the earth . . . a mighty army of prayer warriors."

Known affectionately as "Mother America" by U.S. Aglow members, Sharon became an Aglow member in 1972. She has served in various capacities at Aglow headquarters in Edmonds, Washington, including as assistant to the vice-president of outreach and in the publications department.

In 1980, she became assistant to Aglow's new International President Jane Hansen and in 1981, she was appointed vice-president of the newly created U.S. fellowships department.

Sharon is a sought-after retreat and conference speaker and has earned a reputation as an exhorter, teacher, and encourager of women.

9
...

Persevering (Soaking) Prayer

By Sharon Barrett

There it was, a single sheet of paper containing a testimony of persevering prayer. Something in my heart responded with a resounding "yes!"

Francis MacNutt, the paper's author, was sharing the concept of soaking prayer. He said he felt that almost anyone could be healed of almost anything if God's people were willing to make the spiritual commitment needed to "soak" a person in prayer.

As co-director of Christian Healing Ministries in Florida, the former Catholic priest has spent more than two decades involved with healing of all kinds.

MacNutt gives this definition of soaking prayer: "Soaking prayer conveys the idea of time to let something seep through to the core of something dry that needs to be revived. That's the way it is with the laying on of hands when we feel that God is asking us to take time to irradiate the sickness with his power and love. It is a very gentle prayer."[1]

A Parable of Persistence

We have had much teaching in our day that we only need ask once; anything more shows a lack of faith. However, several places in Scripture indicate God will hear and respond to an ongoing cry of His people.

> Also [Jesus] told them a parable, to the effect that they ought always to pray and not to turn coward— faint, lose heart and give up. He said, In a certain city there was a judge who neither reverenced and feared God nor respected or considered man. And there was a widow in that city who kept coming to him and saying, Protect and defend and give me justice against my adversary. And for a time he would not; but later he said to himself, Though I have neither reverence nor fear of God nor respect or consideration for man, yet because this widow continues to bother me, I will defend and protect and avenge her; lest she give me intolerable annoyance and wear me out by her continual coming, or at the last she come and rail on me, or assault me or strangle me.
>
> Then the Lord said, Listen to what the unjust judge says! And will not [our just] God defend and protect and avenge His elect (His chosen ones) who cry to Him day and night? Will He defer them and delay help on their behalf? (Luke 18:1-7 TAB).

This parable seems to indicate that there are occasions when we need to present our petition more than once. Our

God, who is just, will defend, protect, and avenge His elect who cry out to Him day and night.

MacNutt has experienced hundreds of healings that have taken place over a period of time. He explains it this way, "Suppose we are praying with a person whose hands are crippled with arthritis. I find that such people are occasionally healed dramatically—usually at large prayer meetings. But, for the most part, when I prayed individually for such people, a little improvement would take place: the fingers would straighten a little, the wrist and fingers would be able to bend a little more; often the pain would be reduced or disappear. In short, there would be a noticeable change, but nothing like a complete healing.

"So where do you go from there? . . . Why such a mixed result?

"It was pretty clear that more time for prayer was indicated. I remembered the teachings of Jesus on our need to take time in prayer, to be insistent."[2]

Keep Asking, Keep Knocking

In Matthew 7:7-8 we are told that if we keep on asking, we will receive; if we keep on seeking, we will find; and if we keep on knocking, the door will be opened.

Yet, in western culture particularly, we live in a "microwave" society. We can pop a meal directly from the freezer into the microwave and be eating in ten minutes or less with no real preparation on our part. We've become accustomed to fast food restaurants where we order, eat, and go on our way in less than thirty minutes. Our TV comes on instantly at the touch of a finger with a range of entertainment options available at the click of our channel changer.

Our society gives approval to those who can accomplish several things at once, or who can give "quality minutes" to children and spouses. But when we speak of spending time with Jesus, can we find the depth that we yearn for in a microwave minute?

Unfortunately, it is all too easy for many of us to carry that same "instant" mentality into our prayer life. God urges us gently to spend time with Him.

Our Dual Citizenship

As Christians, we inhabit a visible, sinful world that grows increasingly evil. Yet, the apostle Paul tells us we are also citizens of an invisible spiritual realm. That realm includes us in an ongoing war between God and Satan.

While there is no doubt as to who wins the final battle, God uses the enemy forces coming against us to teach us how to war.

Often we find a parallel between the natural and the spiritual. Ask any soldier who has engaged in a physical battle over contested territory and you will hear stories of how continued bombardment has finally weakened the enemy and caused him to withdraw.

Spiritually, God asks us to do some bombarding on occasion. When one blow alone doesn't fell the enemy, a continuous volley has to weaken him. So it is with soaking prayer for healing. The enemy's grip loosens and he must withdraw.

My Experience with Soaking Prayer

Two years ago, my husband John and I were invited to a home fellowship gathering. One of the women in our group was battling several major illnesses, one of them being cancer.

That night, we gathered around her and someone offered up a prayer. Then the group left her side to continue with the evening's other activities.

Immediately, I felt a grief in my heart because we hadn't taken time to hear God's heart for her. Quietly, I sat at her feet for the next twenty minutes or so. I prayed with my prayer language until I felt a direction on how to pray in English. When I felt I had covered what God wanted for that time, I looked up to see her eyes filled with tears.

"Sharon," she whispered, "you're only the second person in our church who has taken the time to hear God and pray for me."

It was then that I began to believe that the church needed to launch out into committed, soaking prayer if we were going to see the healings that our hearts desire.

To my great surprise, however, I discovered that some were not desirous of this type of prayer because it requires a vulnerability on the part of the recipient as well as those with the prayer team. In this kind of prayer, God may require prayer team members to share areas that need to be corrected in the person's life or to pray in a way that is contrary to their natural mind.

How to Begin Soaking Prayer

Since our early experiences, we have found that soaking prayer teams should consist of several mature Christians who can lead the prayer time and help judge the words that come forth. Others can be newer believers in training. The group should meet at least once a week for no less than an hour.

When someone is sick or in pain, it is difficult for them to have the spiritual energy to pray. The focus of the group needs to be the person in need and all prayer needs to be concentrated in that direction. When the Holy Spirit is in charge, you will be amazed at how each prayer session will take on its own special flavor.

Think how loved you would feel if other Christians surrounded you on a regular basis and carried you through until you received a touch from the Master.

The Commitment of Friends

Mark 2:1-12 tells a poignant love story of friends who cared enough to carry their paralyzed comrade to Jesus for healing. Because of the crowd, they couldn't get him near the Master, so they actually dug through the roof until they had created a hole big enough to lower the paralytic through.

Jesus was impressed with the faith of the paralyzed man's friends and healed him. We can love each other in that same manner today by committing ourselves to do soaking prayer until a breakthrough in health occurs.

Kathy's Story

A friend of mine, Kathy, developed cancer that did not respond to treatment. After three years, her doctor told her to get her house in order as she was down to the final few months of her life.

Without knowing the doctor's verdict, Kathy's close friend, Pat, who had moved to California, felt God calling her to a forty-hour fast. As this had been her previous experience in fasting, she felt comfortable with the request.

At the end of the forty hours, God asked Pat to fast for forty days.

Stunned, she told God she didn't think she could do that. God was silent.

Then Pat asked God to reveal His purpose for the fast. God told her she didn't need to know the purpose. Was she willing? Pat knew the issue was clear: obey or disobey. Because she loved and trusted the Lord, there was no other answer but yes.

She began the fast.

Occasionally the Lord would lead Pat to squeeze some juice from her California citrus trees into water. Pat continued to agree that whatever was on the heart of God would be accomplished.

As Pat's fast continued, Kathy's church youth choir planned a trip to California. They offered the few left-over plane seats to other members of the congregation. Kathy, yearning to see her dear friend, Pat, one last time, obtained permission to make the final trip with some reservations from her doctor.

The doctor warned her not to stumble and to be very careful as the cancer had eaten into her spine and it could be easily fractured. With the doctor's cautions ringing in her ears, Kathy went.

By now, Pat was aware of Kathy's condition when she picked her up at the airport. But Kathy was determined not to let her condition undermine the good time she would share with her friend.

The next day, they obtained a wheelchair and toured the San Diego zoo. The third day it was Sea World.

At about 9 P.M. the next evening, they were at home and decided to put on some Christian tapes. The next thing Pat and Kathy knew, the grandfather clock was striking midnight. Kathy did not know that this midnight hour signified the end of Pat's forty day fast.

Immediately after the clock struck, both women noticed an incredibly bright light coming from across the street. At first they thought someone had turned on a flood light. As they watched, however, the light became a bright ball that crossed the street, came through Pat's house, down the hall, and entered Kathy's body. Instantaneously Kathy fell over on the couch.

As the minutes passed, Kathy was so still that Pat began to wonder if she had died. Finally, Pat walked over and gently touched her but drew her hand back quickly because Kathy's body seemed to radiate heat.

141

Pat's touch brought Kathy back to an awareness of her surroundings. As they sat in the silence, the presence of God was so precious, neither woman spoke. Quietly, they headed for bed.

A while later in her darkened bedroom, Kathy caught a glimpse of light in the mirror and turned to see that it was her own body emitting the glow.

When Kathy awoke the next morning, she was so excited about what happened at midnight that she threw back the covers and leaped out of bed not aware at first of the complete absence of pain in her body.

She threw on her robe, ran to the kitchen where she and Pat began to sort through what had happened. "Did you see . . . what did you feel . . . what exactly . . . ?" Kathy, now fully awake, mentally checked out the places in her body that always hurt. Joyfully, she blurted out that she felt God had healed her completely.

It was only then that Pat understood God's purpose in her forty day fast and rejoiced that He, in His mercy and grace, allowed her to have a part in Kathy's healing.

Kathy flew home and made a doctor's appointment. After he put her through a complete battery of tests, he could only scratch his head at the results. Later, he said that the best way he could describe what the tests showed was that her body seemed to have undergone a sterilizing process that killed virtually all of the cancer.

In this instance of healing, God specifically asked someone to commit herself to fasting and prayer without knowing God's purpose. In His perfect time, God manifested Himself in a powerful way to both Pat and Kathy. Kathy was able to continue her marriage and finish raising her daughters. She is today a living testimony who gives glory to God wherever the story is told.

The Process of Commitment: JoAnn's Story

John and I were leading a fellowship group in our home when we became aware that JoAnn was experiencing an incredible degree of pain due to a neck injury. Her doctors felt she must have had a broken neck at one time and it had gone undiagnosed. Her first vertebra was in sharp, pointed pieces. Moving her head resulted in numbness and excruciating pain throughout her jaw, ear, and temple.

She compensated for the pain by rotating the lower part of her spine which resulted in the vertebrae looking as though they had been pulled out of line to the left side.

While our group was not structured specifically for the purpose of praying for JoAnn, we felt we wanted to undergird her. Each week we set a chair in the middle of the floor and we gathered around to lay hands on our friend. Each week it seemed obvious to us that God was touching her in some way.

After seven months, we needed to take a break. During that time, I was able to ask JoAnn to share with me in greater depth what she had experienced during our prayer times. She said she almost always experienced a physical sensation. Most often she had a sensation of heat, and a feeling that something had been released on the inside.

Sometimes she heard a crackle in her neck as though something were moving. She felt an intense, searing pain in her neck once or twice and a sensation of having been touched at the source of her pain.

JoAnn told us that since we've prayed, she feels a definite difference in the lower part of her spine; she no longer has a major problem in that part of her body.

God Has a Heart to Move

We have dealt with soaking prayer in the arena of

healing, but that is not the only place it can accomplish miracles. It can bind strongholds, set captives free, introduce revival, bring down a Berlin wall, and move the hand of God in astonishing ways.

God has an ear to hear and a heart to move on behalf of His children.

RUTH M. FRIESEN

When Ruth Friesen first heard of Aglow in Victoria, B.C., Canada, it didn't take her long to begin an Aglow in her hometown of Salem, Oregon, in 1972. She served as its first president and later as president of the Salem Evening Aglow for professional women.

Her service opportunities expanded when she became regional director for Oregon, Idaho, and part of Montana, and still later, vice-president of ministries on the national board. She continues her service on Aglow's national board.

This popular retreat and seminar speaker spends much time in the word of God and prayer. "We need to follow the leading of the Holy Spirit, to be much in prayer and His Word, seeking to walk in purity, available and obedient to His will," she says.

10

...

Prayer and the Prophetic

By Ruth M. Friesen

We find all through Scripture that God speaks to us in many different ways. One way is through the gifts of the Holy Spirit.

All of the gifts are valued equally by God with the exception of the greatest gift: love. As Paul says in 1 Corinthians 13, loving others as God loves us is our primary pursuit. That is why the important thing in exercising any of the gifts is to stay focused on God.

Both the first of the Ten Commandments in the Old Testament and the "greatest commandment" spoken by Jesus in Matthew 22:37-40, emphasize this focus. Let me tell you a story that relates perfectly to this kind of natural obedience. A dear friend and missionary in Palentine for thirty-two years once told me that shepherds who take their flocks out to the desert hills for weeks at a time often become lonely. When they can, they meet up with other shepherds, and their flocks mingle.

After fellowship together, the shepherds go their separate ways, each man singing and crooning to his own flock. Incredibly, each sheep hears its own master's voice and follows it without confusion, until the flocks are separated.

That is how I feel about the spiritual gifts God gives us. We need to follow our Master's voice for them to be used without confusion, to His glory.

The Gift of Prophecy

The Word of God gives us several guiding principles for the purpose and ministry of prophecy:

The gift of prophecy is one of the gifts for "edification, exhortation and comfort" (1 Cor. 14:3). It comes only by the anointing and inspiration of the Holy Spirit. Often, its main purpose is to build up the saints as they are gathered together.

Paul tells us in First Corinthians 12 that we are not to be ignorant concerning spiritual gifts. We are to seek the Lord as the Holy Spirit reveals Him in all His glory and quickens our spirits to be available and obedient to His nudging.

The Thompson Chain Reference Bible says under the heading Religious Officials, Old Testament:

"The Prophet—Men divinely called and inspired to deliver God's message, particularly in relation to future events. In the New Testament, the word *prophet* refers to a person who had received a special spiritual gift enabling him to interpret or proclaim Truth, and does not necessarily involve the element of predictions."

148

Prophecy as Confirmation

There are times when the Holy Spirit anoints a person to give a prophetic word at a given time for a specific person or for a group of people. This is the heart of God conveying His desires to them at that particular time and may be a confirmation of a word He has already revealed to their hearts, rather than a prediction as such.

Let me illustrate this: Some time ago during a convention, the Lord gave me a song in tongues and interpretation. After the meeting, a gentleman asked if he could meet the Jewish lady who sang the song. I told him I was not Jewish, nor did I know Hebrew. Puzzled, he asked me how I knew the Hebrew chant that he had sung in a Jewish synagogue for seven years.

This man, now a Christian, had come to the convention to hear more about the charismatic movement. God confirmed his experience with my song, which helped to convince him of the genuine move and presence of God. He went home and shared his experience in his church and many received the baptism of the Holy Spirit.

God had drawn this man to hear about the ministry of the gifts of the Spirit, and I was merely the vessel the Holy Spirit used to confirm the truth of the gifts to him.

Only God Chooses His Vessels for Prophecy

Someone who moves in prophetic words can be highly educated or illiterate. Second Timothy 2:20, 21 says that God looks for a vessel he can use. There are vessels of gold and silver, also of wood and clay, some for honor and some for dishonor. If a person purges himself from the latter, he shall be a vessel unto honor, sanctified for the Master's use, and prepared for every good work. We need to remember that the vessel being used is not supernatural, but the message is the supernatural word of the Holy Spirit and must always bring the focus to Jesus Christ and our heavenly Father.

Once, a little woman prophesied at a meeting one evening that God was in their midst to deliver and heal a certain person. Everyone knew she was illiterate, but as she spoke in obedience to the glory of God, a miracle of healing immediately took place for the person needing deliverance. Because God looks on the heart, she was a vessel unto honor.

Words in Spiritual Language Must Be Interpreted

First Corinthians 14:27-31 says, "If anyone speaks in a tongue, let there be two or at the most three, each in turn and let one interpret. But if there is no interpreter, let him keep silent in church."

Prophecy Agrees with the Written Word

A prophetic word should always be in accordance with the written Word of God, never contrary to God's character, ways, or principles. If it is contrary in any aspect, a believer should refuse to receive or move upon it.

Usually a true word will confirm what the Holy Spirit is speaking to that person's heart, like fresh manna given in the wilderness daily for the need. A fresh and inspired word will come at the right time. In the word given, a person may get some direction or an answer to her prayer or heart's longing. It should never draw attention to the person operating in the gift.

The person receiving a prophetic word should know that she herself must seek God with regard to what was spoken and be obedient to His leading and guidance.

Orderliness in Prophecy

As Paul states in 1 Corinthians 14:29, two or three prophets should speak during a meeting while the others judge the authenticity of the prophetic utterances, in order to preserve balance and prevent confusion during a meeting or worship service.

Words of Prophecy, Wisdom, Knowledge Work Together

A "word of knowledge," a "word of wisdom," or a prophetic word often are intertwined as the Holy Spirit brings forth God's desire for a specific purpose and time. The Holy Spirit knows what is the best gift for the person receiving the gift. It may be healing, a word of knowledge, a word of wisdom, or more than one gift at a time.

Again, God's desire is for us to mature and be strong in ministering any gift, showing forth His power. First Corinthians 14:12 says, "Since you are zealous for spiritual gifts, let it be for the edification of the church that you seek to excel."

To Those Who Exercise Prophetic Gifts

If you move in the gift of prophecy, it is important to be obedient in yielding to the Holy Spirit's prompting. The Holy Spirit will anoint and inspire you to speak out that which the Father God's heart is wanting to convey to the group gathered together.

However, it is wise to not always be the one to give the inspired message, but, in honor, allow others to move in the exercise of such gifts, submitting to other members of the body. Wait quietly and prayerfully, being available to be used if need be.

If you have recently received the gift of prophecy, it is

wise to learn to yield to the Holy Spirit in a smaller gathering until you feel comfortable. The gifts should flow naturally in a tone of voice that can be heard clearly, for all to be edified.

A prophetic word given should never introduce a crosscurrent of thought to what was already introduced. Rather, the gifts of the Spirit should flow in the direction the Spirit is leading the body of believers into. The presence of the Lordship of Jesus is paramount as each heart seeks to hear His voice. For as the spiritual tide rises, it will be felt by the whole body if the members are in tune with the working of the Holy Spirit.

When I Was a Child

A holy awe and reverence of the presence and move of the Holy Spirit was planted in me as early as age five, when the gifts of the Holy Spirit were manifested during our services at church.

I was the middle child of ten children. We all loved to have family worship at home in the morning and evening. As Dad led us in worship, I soon learned to talk to God at a very early age. More than saying prayers, I just talked to Him. This helped me to realize how personal, close, and loving my Father God was. He was always there.

And Jesus seemed so real to me! Even though I gave my heart to Him when I was six years old, I felt that I belonged to God for as long as I could remember.

I was awed at the thought that He was so faithful and obedient to die for me. Thus, over many years of longing to know Him better, I became sensitive to the wooing of the Holy Spirit and to the voice of God.

By the time I became a teenager, I could hardly wait for the church young people's meetings on Tuesday nights. After the service, we would gather around the altar to pray. Week after week, month after month, we would be startled that the clock showed it was midnight or after. We would have to quit praying and go home.

When I was around age fifteen, the pastor and his wife invited me to stay one night after the others left and continue to pray with them. Later, I spent the night at their home.

That night, I finally said, "Jesus, all I want is YOU," and with a sudden gentleness I was enveloped in His presence. My English language no longer had the words to express my overwhelming love and adoration for my Lord. New syllables began to take form in my mouth. I struggled to keep myself in control and get out words that I knew, but I felt like I would burst if I didn't let the new words come. When I yielded, the language flowed so freely, that after awhile I had to stop and declare, "Now, Lord, you know what I have been really trying to tell you!"

I knew that I was communing with my Lord in a new way, and I could finally express my deep love and my heart secrets to Him. That night, I began a lifetime of a fresh longing to know Him in an ever increasing and deeper way.

The Greatest Teacher

Even then, God was teaching me that I could choose to yield and be obedient or choose not to step out of my safety zone where my exercise of His gifts was concerned.

Before any service or meeting I always felt led to pray, "Lord, if this is your desire, then please make a place and time that I am to speak." I still marvel at how the Holy Spirit always makes His time and place for a word to be given.

It was very hard for me at first because I had to fight a feeling of shyness. Yet, if I didn't yield to the prompting of the Holy Spirit, there was always a feeling of being sorry that I hadn't obeyed. But when I did obey Him, there was the wonderful feeling of pleasing Him.

Years ago I asked a minister friend to pray that God would release me from the fear of people. God answered his prayer but my deliverence from fear was not immediate. Many times I had to quote the scripture, "I can do all things through Christ who strengthens me" (Phil. 4:13). His Word has changed me!

Prophetic Words in Healing

Some years ago when my husband and I held regular home meetings for ministry to our community, the wife of a Presbyterian pastor came from a sick bed to receive healing. She came even though she was somewhat afraid of being in the presence of our charismatic form of ministry.

Yet, when we prayed for her, she was very disappointed because nothing seemed to happen. Before she left, a few of us joined hands again and just prayed for her in the Spirit. Just then, I heard myself speaking in words that sounded very oriental.

As soon as I was through, I saw her smiling with relief. "My dear," she said, "you were speaking in Mandarin Chinese. My father was Jonathan Goforth, a missionary to China. He preached in Mandarin and had great revivals in his time." She went on to say that God had just spoken to her spirit, telling her she had nothing to fear. Rather, she was to trust His love for her and to receive the gifts of healing He was bringing to her.

That night, she was wonderfully touched by Jesus, the great physician, as the Holy Spirit distributed the best gift for her need. She was completely healed.

Prophetic Words of Warning

The Holy Spirit often prompts us to pray when we do not know the need or reason. As we pray in the Spirit, we may see in our mind's eye a certain circumstance that is occurring or about to occur. Then we can take authority over the powers of darkness and speak a prophetic word into the situation through the name of Jesus and the power of His shed blood. Gloriously, we see God move into the situation by His power.

A few years ago, I was asked to speak at an Aglow meeting on the Oregon coast. A severe storm of hurricane proportions was predicted and every few minutes on radio and TV, broadcasters warned people to stay off the mountain roads because of falling trees. I had a three-hour drive ahead of me.

Still, I felt I was to go. So I prayed, speaking directly to the elements, the winds, and rain. I reminded them that Jesus had taken authority over the winds and storm, speaking peace, and that the prince of the air and all the elements are still subject to the power of His name. I commanded the storm, in Jesus' name, to go back out to sea and come in way up the coast if it had to. We completed our trip and had a wonderful meeting.

It was only when we arrived home and picked up the newspaper that we saw the headlines, "Strange phenomenon! Storm suddenly turns out to sea and comes back in much further up the coast."

Another example of the need to yield to the Spirit's still small voice of warning occurred while I was driving on a road with several dangerous curves. The thought entered my mind to be careful of a car coming head-on around a corner and hitting me. I should have prayed and taken authority right then; instead, I continued to think about it.

Very shortly after, a car did round the corner on the wrong side, heading straight for me. I barely had time to say, "Jesus!" just before the driver swerved back to his side of the road.

155

Women of Prayer

We need to be aware that many, many times the Holy Spirit may be prophetically revealing a scene in our minds, even if it seems like just an ordinary thought. As we take authority over the revealed situation and pray in Jesus' name or even shout His name alone, God can intervene.

Prophetic Role Models

James 5:17-18 records Elijah's prophetic prayer that it might not rain. Elijah prayed again and the heavens gave rain and the earth brought forth its fruit after a three-and-a-half year drought. When a prophetic word is given under the inspiration of the Holy Spirit, we need to follow through and pray earnestly that God's will will be carried out.

According to Joshua 10:12-14, Joshua spoke a word (prophetic prayer) and commanded the sun to stand still while they finished their battle with the enemy. The Bible says there was no day like that before or after.

I like the example Elisha sets in 1 and 2 Kings as he follows Elijah. He leaves all and follows with great determination and energy. He was a man of great integrity. He lived in a spirit of victory. He was a man of spiritual vision. He would not be denied, but followed Elijah with all his heart, mind, and soul.

• He asked for a double portion of Elijah's spirit and received it.

• He saw Elijah taken up in a chariot of fire. He picked up Elijah's mantle and went forth in authority and power as Elijah had done.

• He did even greater things than what had been done before.

Let us follow our Lord with the same determination.

God is looking for a people who will know Him through prayer and whose hearts are perfect toward Him that He might show Himself strong in their behalf.

In Sorrow, Uplifting Words

In December, 1992, my husband fell, injuring his head badly. Even as he lay in the Neuro Intensive Care Unit of the hospital over Christmas Day, the Holy Spirit was faithful to prepare my heart for my husband's home going. Every night, I would wake up to the music of a hymn going through my mind. As I tried to remember the words of the tune, it seemed to bring a comforting prophetic message each time:

What have I to dread,
What have I to fear,
Leaning on the everlasting arms?
I have perfect peace,
With my Lord so near,
Leaning on the everlasting arms.

The Hallelujah Chorus was playing in my husband's hospital room on Christmas Day. The glory of the Lord seemed to fill it. Later in the day, when a pastor came in to pray with us, he said, "Ruth, I must tell you . . . the words come to me so strongly, "And the glory shone around."

During the last two days of my husband's life on earth, again, I felt the comfort of the prophetic word through a song given by the Holy Spirit.

Lead me gently home, Father,
Lead me gently home . . .

Several other families with loved ones in our unit felt the peace of Jesus around us and asked us about it. Thanks be to God, three of them gave their hearts to Him.

Calling to Prayer

There has been a great calling to prayer around the world during the last few years. The cry of the Holy Spirit today is for the Church, the Body of Christ, to repent, be purified, anointed, and empowered. Truly the fields are ripe for harvest.

Joel 2:28 says, "I will pour out My spirit on all flesh; your sons and your daughters shall prophesy. . . ." These are the days when we need to see the Word go forth in the power and demonstration of the mighty Holy Spirit.

Section III

Released to the Nations

The Power of Prayer

MARFA CABRERA

Argentinean Marfa Cabrera has been a member of Aglow since 1981 and her leadership roles in the fellowship have encompassed local, national, and international offices.

She has been a local president, national coordinator, and outreach director to South America. At present, she serves as a member of Aglow's International Board of Directors.

Married to pastor and evangelist Omar Cabrera, Marfa remembers one of many profound times of prayer when God "inhabited the praises of His people."

"When our ministry was under tremendous financial pressure, and my husband nearly gave up, I had an idea—surely inspired by the Holy Spirit—to start daily prayer meetings early in the morning with a small group of members in our church. We prayed for about twenty days, interceding and doing spiritual warfare. Then the Lord told us to start worshipping Him and giving Him thanks for what He had already done.

"The astonishing thing was that he reversed our situation just five days after we began giving thanks. One month later, we not only paid all the church's debts, we had money in the bank!"

11

...

Praying and Fasting for the Lost

By Marfa Cabrera

When He came to the disciples, He saw a great multitude around them, and the scribes disputing with them.

Immediately when they saw Him, all the people were greatly amazed and running to Him greeted Him.

And He asked the scribes, "What are you discussing with them?"

Then one from the multitude answered and said, "Teacher, I brought You my son, who has a mute spirit.

"And whenever he seizes him, he throws him down; he foams at the mouth, gnashes his teeth and becomes rigid. So I spoke to your disciples that they should cast him out, but they could not."

He answered them and said, "O faithless generation, how long shall I be with you? How long shall I bear with you? Bring him to Me."

Then they brought him to Him. And when he saw Him, immediately the spirit convulsed him and he fell on the ground and wallowed, foaming at the mouth.

So He asked his father, "How long has this been happening to him?" And he said, "From childhood.

"And often he has thrown him both into the fire and into the water to destroy him. But if You can do anything, have compassion on us and help us."

Jesus said to him, "If you can believe all things are possible to him who believes."

Immediately the father of the child cried out and said with tears, "Lord I believe; help my unbelief!"

When Jesus saw that the people came running together, He rebuked the unclean spirit, saying to him, "You deaf and dumb spirit, I command you, come out of him, and enter him no more!"

Then the spirit cried out, convulsed him greatly and came out of him. And he became as one dead so that many said, "He is dead."

But Jesus took him by the hand and lifted him up, and he arose.

And when He had come into the house, His disciples asked Him privately, "Why could we not cast him out?"

So He said to them, "This kind can come out by nothing but prayer and fasting" (Mark 9:14-29).

A Father's Love

Our hearts become tender when we picture a father suffering for his beloved son tormented by the forces of darkness that seek to damage the boy. In this passage it is very evident that satanic legions are fighting to destroy him entirely—this human being whom God created.

Our hearts momentarily sink with despair to see that Jesus' disciples cannot help this man or even soothe his torment. But they revive with hope when Jesus Christ, the Son of God, appears on the scene. He who has all power in heaven and on earth pierces the tormenting darkness with His presence. He, before whom every knee shall bow, uses His authority: a glorious, complete deliverance takes place.

Later, privately, the disciples ask Jesus, " Why couldn't we set him free?" In other words, "What is the secret to victory in such a case?"

In this situation, unbelief was the stumbling block that stopped the miracle. Jesus said to the disciples, "Oh unbelieving generation. . . ." On the other hand, He told the young man's father, "If you can believe, everything is possible."

Jesus' answer teaches us clearly that spiritual powers of darkness can only be overcome by spiritual powers of light. We open the way for the power of light through prayer and fasting.

Reasons for Fasting

Unfortunately, fasting has not been considered important in the church for some time, but there are several sound, biblical reasons for fasting. I believe that since the Holy Spirit is restoring all things, He is also calling each of us in His Body to a deeper commitment in this area.

Some reasons for fasting are

• Fasting is a river of great spiritual power, a means of victory when the people of God are faced with crises, persecutions, changes, satanic strongholds, personal and national needs. It is a powerful weapon, an instrument of deliverance.

165

• Fasting with prayer is a place where God can cause a change to occur in us; we place ourselves where God's blessings can reach us.

• Fasting is the cure to unbelief. (Reread Mark 9:14-29).

When we back our prayers with fasting, our faith develops and grows. Then, "everything is possible to him who believes."

• Fasting is a great spiritual adventure where we open a way for the power of light to overcome the darkness.

• Prayer with fasting brings a harvest of souls into the kingdom of God. As evangelist Reinhard Bonke is fond of saying, "Fasting empties hell and populates heaven."

In times when only a miracle can be the answer to a given situation, fasting is always one of the most effective ways to see the power of the Lord moving mountains on behalf of His people. Some of the greatest breakthroughs I have seen in my walk with God have been in answer to prayer with fasting.

When we take time to study Scripture, we see over and over again that fasting is the means to victory. In ancient times prophets, kings, and the people of God fasted when faced with crises, personal and national.

Here are some examples:

Individuals

Ahab	1 Kings 21: 27-29
Ezra	Ezra 10: 6-17
David	Psalms 35:13, 69:10
Daniel	Daniel 9:3, 20-27
Esther	Esther 4:13-16
Darius	Daniel 6:18-24
Paul	Acts 9:9-17
Jesus	Matthew 4:1-11

Groups of People

Nineveh	Nehemiah 1:4; 2:10
Jews	Esther 4:1-3
John's disciples	Matthew 9:14-15
Church at Antioch	Acts 13:1-5
Paul and others	Acts 27:33

Jesus of Nazareth, our Master and Teacher, gave us a powerful example. He was taken by the Holy Spirit to the desert to fast for forty days before starting His public ministry. There He overcame temptation and the devil.

In God's Eyes . . .

In God's eyes, the motivation for fasting is more important than the physical sacrifice. The Lord looks upon the heart. If we have a bad attitude or there are selfish motives, the fast will be spiritually ineffective. It is of no use to fast and pray, asking the Lord to make us compassionate, understanding, and capable of giving a word of encouragement, and yet complain about our situation, our relatives and neighbors, find faults in our husbands or in our children, see only flaws in those around us.

Fasting should bring us to the place where we, by faith, see the good and the positive in others, forgiving, accepting, loving them, and wanting every possible blessing and victory in their lives. "Then [our] light will rise in the darkness, and [our] night will become like the noonday" (Isa. 58:10 NIV).

Historical Examples

All through human history, the great men of faith practiced fasting. The prayer warrior of the last century, John Hyde, also known as "Praying Hyde," was such a man. A friend relates, "It was evident to all he was bowed down with sore travail of soul. He missed many meals and when I went to his room I would find him lying as in great agony, or walking up and down as if an inward fire were burning in his bones."[1]

Praying Hyde's intense burden for souls prompted him to ask God for one soul a day for a year. At the year's end, four hundred souls were won to Christ. The next year, Hyde approached God's throne begging for two souls a day, then four. He became a burden-bearer for mankind, but his calling was not to win these in massive crusades. He went for every person one at a time.[2]

What Is Fasting?

Fasting, or not eating, is a spiritual exercise, when the time in which we normally eat, is set aside for prayer and meditation. To fast is to tell God, "Lord, today I hunger for you; I need you more than I need food, my soul needs to be filled with your power more than my body needs the physical energy." Fasting has real meaning and value when time is taken to pray.

There are many who believe that fasting and "to be hungry" are the same thing. Fasting is neither a hunger strike, through which we are trying to blackmail God into doing what we want, twisting His arm into changing His mind about something we desire, nor is it action that gets God to feel sorry for us. It does not mean that if we fast, God is going to change His will or that He is forced to give us what we ask for.

Food caused the fall of mankind; fasting humbles the soul before God and crucifies the appetites and desires of the flesh. Fasting manifests our deep desire to be with the Master and to know His will, to the point that we are willing to leave everything else aside in order to seek His face and obey Him. This is the heart attitude of fasting which brings sanctification, consecration, and humility.

It is during these times when we seek His will that God shows us the changes and adjustments that each one of us has to make personally in order that His blessings will not be restrained by our attitudes or our sin. Rather, through obeying and pleasing Him, His blessings flow unhindered.

The Basis for Fasting

The Word of God declares,

> Is not this the kind of fasting I have chosen: to loose the chains of injustice and untie the cords of the yoke, to set the oppressed free and break every yoke? Is it not to share your food with the hungry and to provide the poor wanderer with shelter—when you see the naked, to clothe him and not to turn away from your own flesh and blood? Then your light will break forth like the dawn, and your healing will quickly appear; then your righteousness will go before you, and the glory of the Lord will be your rear guard.
> *Then you will call and the Lord will answer; you will cry for help and he will say: Here am I.*
> If you do away with the yoke of oppression, with the pointing finger and malicious talk, and if you spend yourselves on behalf of the hungry and satisfy the needs of the oppressed, then your light will rise in the darkness, and your night will become like the noonday (Isa. 58:6-10 NIV).

It is fasting like this that the Lord chose as a means for His people to receive powerful answers, fasting that changes us from the inside out, that shows our heart of compassion.

The Bible tells us that when Barnabas and Paul "ministered to the Lord and fasted," the Holy Spirit spoke, "Separate to me Barnabas and Saul for the work to which I have called them" (Acts 13:2). Only then did the disciples lay hands on them, pray for them, and send them to preach.

Take note that Paul and Barnabas did not organize a farewell party with lots of food and drink; they began one of the greatest missionary endeavors in history, and they began it by fasting.

Every Christian should practice fasting, particularly those in some kind of ministry who want to see the anointing increase in their service to the King.

How Long? How Frequently?

The Word of God doesn't always say how long people fasted, but we do have the report that some fasted one day, others for three days, seven days, fourteen days, twenty-one days. The Bible records that Moses, Joshua, Elijah, and Jesus each fasted forty days. Each of us needs to determine our desires, needs, physical strength; we also need to examine how hungry we are to see God move in a supernatural way.

Sad to say, many of the benefits of fasting are still unknown to most Christians today. There is a great source of spiritual energy in fasting. It has always been an efficient way to receive power from God over all the powers of the enemy.

Types of Fasting

Several types of fasting are illustrated in the Word of God, including the following:

• Public Fasting

When a national leader, prophet, or servant of God, faced with a national crisis or any other situation that may

170

affect a people, calls for a fast, he sets a specific day or time for a nation, a city or a group of people to fast with one accord. (See Esther 4:1-3; Acts 13:1-5).

• **Private Fasting**

When someone presents a personal prayer request to the Lord or simply takes time to seek God on behalf of someone else or some situation that needs divine intervention.

• **Regularly Scheduled Fasting**

When a person or group fasts on a regular basis. This is what Aglow practices every Thursday. Women around the world who are of "one heartbeat" set this time aside to fast and pray, to intercede before the Lord for the many diverse needs within the Aglow ministry, its leaders, and other individuals as well as for the outreach and vision of Aglow.

• **Occasional Fasting**

When an unforeseen need comes up and we decide to fast, or when we get up one morning and our spiritual hunger surpasses our physical desire to eat.

• **Voluntary Fasting**

When we plan in advance to take one or more days to intercede for a given situation, need, or activity in the ministry.

• **Habit-breaking Fasting**

I have heard of giving up something that we really enjoy or think that we cannot do without for a day or a certain period of time. For example, not drinking coffee, not watching television, or not eating a favorite food.

• **Medical Fasting**

For years some doctors have advised their patients to fast for a day to give their bodies a rest. As we fast, our blood circulates more freely and our minds work more clearly. Occasionally these doctors recommend that certain patients fast for a week because of fasting's healing powers as a therapy that opens the pores, clears the lungs, cleans the kidneys and intestines, and sharpens the senses, especially taste and smell, and greatly improves mental faculties.

Science and experience have proved that in order to survive, every human being needs four elements: air, water, sleep, and food. Without air you can only survive minutes. Without water or sleep, a few days. However, without food, several weeks.

Practical Tips

The time you set aside to fast varies according to your individual physical strength and the urgency and magnitude of the need. You can fast until the afternoon or evening or until the next day. It is an agreement between you and God, no one else.

If you feel God is calling you to fast for several days, you should plan in advance to cease from some of your regular activities so you have plenty of time to be in the presence of the Lord, praying with no rush, waiting to hear His voice.

It is always advisable to drink plenty of liquids such as fruit juices or water, especially if you have to continue with a normal schedule. (Diabetics and others who need regular nourishment for medical reasons, should heed the advice of their physicians).

If you are a first-time faster, you may face physical discomforts, such as increased appetite, headaches, feeling weak or dizzy. Usually, these symptoms can be overcome with prayer. You will be able to fast for longer periods of time with practice.

Jesus recommends, "When you fast, put oil on your head and wash your face, so that it will not be obvious to men that you are fasting, but only to your Father, who is unseen; and your Father, who sees what is done in secret, will reward you" (Matt. 6:17-18 NIV). Let's not transmit our sacrifice in fasting by looking pitiful to others; rather, with enthusiasm, we need to show the happiness and joy of having a special time of fellowship with the Lord.

During the days that you set aside to fast, use different types of prayers: worship . . . communion and praise . . . intercessory prayer . . . prayer of authority . . . warfare . . . silence.

In those times when Satan tries to tempt you with despondency, rebuke him in the name of Jesus, and begin to praise the Lord. When we fast, we are in a battle, but it is not a struggle "against flesh and blood, but against the rulers, against the authorities, against the powers of this dark world and against the spirit forces of evil in the heavenly realms" (Eph. 6:12 NIV).

The Greatest Secrets

I learned the greatest secrets of praying and fasting for the lost years ago from my husband Omar.

Before we got married, both of us had studied very hard and with great enthusiasm in Bible school to prepare ourselves for the ministry. During our first pastorate, we were sorely disappointed when we took a church with only twelve very poor, uneducated people in it. We did not know what kind of a program to develop with this small, impoverished little group. Nevertheless, we worked hard. But our frustration increased because we saw few results.

When Omar was ready to give up, the Holy Spirit showed him a way out: One day he decided to try fasting.

He began to fast from Friday to Sunday night. After several weeks passed, several influential people in town who had come to hear him preach, got saved. They, in turn, drew others. Soon we had approximately 120 people attending our church. With that group, my husband organized

173

a city wide crusade. When he enlisted the participation of other churches, all the other pastors felt a crusade would not work, so Omar decided to go for it alone.

He began a fast as the crusade started and the fast continued for forty-five days. During that time, he was led by the Holy Spirit into spiritual warfare and learned how to bring down strongholds and the strongman in a certain area.

It was only then that his ministry exploded and he began to reach multitudes. Thousands who attended that crusade gave their lives to Jesus. Tremendous healings resulted and a big church was established. The spiritual atmosphere had been cleansed through fasting and praying.

Omar's Season of Fasting

Ever since that time, Omar periodically sets a time of prayer and fasting for the purpose of reaching the lost. When God shows him a particular city, and his team is in the final stages of planning a crusade, Omar locks himself in a hotel room to be alone with God. The first thing he does is to keep the radio and television turned off and leave aside all reading material except the Word of God.

On such occasions, by mutual agreement, we take separate rooms because his entire time is set apart, dedicated toward praying and going into spiritual warfare in order to see thousands come into the kingdom.

Omar says that the greatest challenge during fasting is to submit himself to the lordship of Jesus Christ, to empty himself of everything else in order to be filled with Jesus Christ's compassion and authority. Getting to this point takes several days of constant surrender and renouncement; it is not easy to bring his mind under the control of the Holy Spirit. This cannot be rushed.

The struggle begins at the point when he begins to seek God and His power on behalf of the lost. All kinds of things he should be doing come to his mind: He should be writing a letter to the workers and ministers, making a phone call to someone who is sick, working on the book he never has time to finish. As he goes through this process, Omar says the minutes seem like hours. Just when he thinks he's prayed for the better part of a day for everything and everyone, a glance at his watch tells him only a few minutes have gone by.

Yet, he continues to ask the Lord to empty him of self in order to receive instructions from God. Those instructions are very important because they contain information on how to penetrate darkness, discern, and bring down the strongman and set the captives free.

The struggle goes on.

His passion to see the lost saved has to get stronger than all the good ideas and desires, stronger than hunger and sleep. It has to get to the point where the soul in agony breaks the dimension of human time, and cries out to God in complete surrender to His divine will.

Then the breakthrough takes place.

Omar says it is like going from one dimension into another, from the natural to the supernatural. All of a sudden, the flesh, mind, and time no longer have control over him. Only then do the hours become minutes as he stands, sits, or lies prostrate in the presence of the Almighty God, and his spirit fellowships with His.

Only then is it time to take authority in the name of Jesus and begin to weaken the strongholds of darkness and the devil in the lives of lost souls. This becomes such an exciting task when he experiences the reverse of his beginning perception about time. Praying absorbs him so completely he senses that only few minutes have gone by when, in fact, hours have passed and tremendous power has been released.

Power to Transform

What Omar has experienced of the power of God through fasting is open to any believer who has a heart that yearns to follow hard after the Lord. We know that without Christ, men and women are spiritually dead. What a glorious victory it is to see others set free as a result of time we spend in fasting and prayer.

It is my prayer that each one of us will receive from the Holy Spirit the vision and faith necessary to pray and fast so that the power of God to touch and transform lives will be greatly manifested. Let us join the army of those who have learned that some answers can only be obtained through fasting with prayer. Our lives will be enriched by this experience.

PAT CHEN

Pat Chen, an ordained minister, has served Aglow in local, area, national, and international capacities since 1975. Currently, she is a member of Aglow's International Prayer Council.

Pat was president of her local Aglow in Maryland before she served as president of the Maryland West Area Board. She helped found two locals in Maryland. Pat became a U.S. field representative in 1988 and served on Aglow's U.S. and international boards from 1990-1992.

Pat remembers that her first exposure to committed prayer came particularly through Naomi Frasca and Margaret Thomas, members of her local fellowship. "They were mighty, powerful, full of faith. When they prayed, people got saved, healed, delivered, filled. They had an intimate walk with Jesus. That is my vision for Aglow and for women everywhere: that they would walk humbly, as these women did, but with power."

Pat believes the Lord has called her to be a reconciler and unifier within Aglow and the Body of Christ. "He has shown me that He wants to use Aglow women to be a significant part of revival. God has spoken to my heart about using me to stir up within women a heart that pants after Him."

Pat is married to Peter Chen and they have one son, Kenon.

12

• • •

Tools for Prayer: Maps and Strategies

By Pat Chen

I will never be the same!

I have met God. I have felt His touch. I have heard His voice. I have seen His face. He has healed and continues to heal the very core of my being.

A Vision for the World

When I cried out to Him, "I want to know You. I want to know Your presence in a greater way. I want Your fire. I want to feel Your heartbeat. What is on Your heart, Lord?" He answered, "People."

People are on the heart of God.

Fresh Anointing

A few years ago, on my departure day from an Aglow conference, I felt a desperate need to stay in the hotel room, praying and worshipping the Lord. One of my roommates, Jayne Young, an area board president at the time, took one look at me and knew God was saying that it wasn't time to go. It was time to pray.

As she prayed for the world, the anointing for intercession fell upon her in a way I have not often heard or seen on others since. She literally went around the globe in prayer. Simultaneously, I had a vision of what she prayed. I saw the world, the people of all colors and languages, their dress, and most of all, their need for Jesus.

As I saw this, I repented with deep sobs and my body shook under the conviction and power of God. I said, "Father, forgive me, for I have forgotten these people." After my repentance, Jayne prayed for a visit from God as on the Day of Pentecost. God touched my hands, my feet, my mouth, my heart.

Since that day, hours in prayer seem like moments to me. Fasting has become a lifestyle led by His Holy Spirit. There is not enough paper or time to tell it all.

Maps as a Daily Prayer Tool

Back at home, when I began laying my hands on a map of the United States as I prayed, I found myself weeping and, at times, in deep travail as I cried out to God for revival. As I prayed for each state by name, I would break the enemy's hold and claim Psalm 85:6-7, "Will you not revive us again, that your people may rejoice in you? Show us your unfailing love, O Lord, and grant us your salvation" (NIV).

For years now on a daily basis, I have prayed for nations, their leaders, and major Christian organizations as I use

Tools for Prayer: Maps and Strategies

The World Prayer Map designed by Dick Eastman, president of Every Home for Christ, (formerly Change the World Ministries). Using this map, I can see where the Communist, Marxist, Socialist, Moslem, and free nations are located. Therefore, I know better how to pray for them. It has became a blessed tool in my prayer closet.

Aglow's first world prayer map, created in 1993, emphasizes praying through the "10/40 window." Islam, Buddhism, and Hinduism, the three major religious blocs in the world are within countries that lie between the 10th and 40th degrees latitude north of the equator, or the "10/40 window." Here, two-thirds of the world's people live in one-third of the world's land mass: the poorest people with the lowest literacy, the lowest life expectancy, and the highest infant mortality.

Ninety-seven percent of the least evangelized live here, yet less than thirty percent of the world's missionaries serve in these "10/40 window" countries now. The reasons? Many of these countries, particularly Islamic nations, have been openly hostile to Christian witness. It is difficult, often dangerous missionary work.

Occasionally, we all have been like reluctant warriors who would like to escape war and confrontation with the enemy if we could. However, just as there were seasons appointed for war in biblical times, we are to be obedient to God as willing warriors engaging in spiritual warfare, using a map as a tool to accomplish God's purposes.

All of God's servants do not necessarily have the same call and "burden" to pray for or minister in the same cities or nations. Some intercessors are called to pray with great fervency for their church, local community, and the city that surrounds their church. Others are called by God to pray with a special focus on their state or country. Still others are ignited by God to pray for the world with a special heart interest in specific nations. Ezekiel's target burden given to him by the Lord was Jerusalem.

Ezekiel, Man of the Map

And you, son of man, take a tile and lay it before you, and make upon it a drawing of a city, even Jerusalem.

And put siege-works against it, and build a siege-wall against it, and cast up a mound against it; set camps also against it, and set battering rams against it round about.

Moreover take a plate of iron and place it for an iron wall between you and the city; and set your face toward it, and it shall be besieged, and you shall press the siege against it. This is a sign to the house of Israel (Ezek. 4:1-3 TAB).

Ezekiel was one of the most interesting and colorful prophets in the Old Testament. Amos 3:7 states, "Surely the Lord God does nothing unless He reveals His secret counsel to His servants the prophets."

Ezekiel, prophet and priest, was also called a watchman.

Called as a Watchman

In the Old Testament, a watchman was a sentinel or guard. He was to keep watch over and guard the city, warning others of impending danger. Irijah, who kept watch at the Benjamin Gate, is referred to in Scripture as the "lord of oversight" or "captain of the guard," in Jeremiah 37:13.

Some watchmen were stationed like policemen on the city streets. Others were posted on the fortified walls of a city. Still others stood on a watchtower or a command post on a hill in the wilderness.

Our Call to Establish Spiritual Command Posts

Our modern cities no longer have watchmen, yet in Habakkuk we have a clear model of our role as spiritual watchmen over our homes, our neighborhoods, and our cities. The prophet stood on his "spiritual rampart," so to speak, to look and listen for what God had to say about his nation (2:1).

Only the Most High God can surround anyone or a nation with a hedge of protection by His Spirit through our prayers. We are admonished that, "Unless the Lord builds the house, they labor in vain who build it; unless the Lord guards the city, the *watchman* stays awake in vain" (Ps. 127:1). The Hebrew word for *guard* and *watchman* in this passage is "shamar." It means, "to hedge about" (as with thorns) i.e. guard; protect, attend to, be circumspect, take heed (to self), keep, mark, look narrowly, observe, preserve, regard, reserve, save and wait (for).

Let us always keep the scriptural focus that it is "not by might nor by power, but by My Spirit, says the Lord of Hosts" (Zech. 4:6).

A Watchman's Job Description

Interestingly, this same Hebrew word for watchman in Psalm 127, *shamar*, is used in Genesis 2:15 where the Lord took Adam and put him in the garden to cultivate and keep it. *Shamar* is also used in Genesis 3:24 when the cherubim had to *keep* man out and *guard* the way to the tree of life. In these scriptures lies a simple job description of a watchman over a city. He is to help keep the enemy (Satan) out of the garden and guard against the fleshly intervention of man who would come against the progress of the kingdom of God being built here on earth.

The word *watchman* in Ezekiel 3:17 has a corresponding meaning: God was appointing Ezekiel "to lean forward," i.e. to peer into the distance; by implication to observe, await, and watch.

Basically, he was being called by the Lord to go beyond what he could easily see on the surface with the naked eye. He was being asked to look into the invisible realm—to be a "spiritual spy." He was to search out, examine, and obtain as much information as possible in order to warn God's people.

The translation of *warn* in verse 17 is to gleam, to enlighten (by caution), admonish, and teach. Therefore, after Ezekiel was informed by God of the moral condition of Israel, he was responsible to caution them against their sinful ways so that they would have an opportunity to repent and escape judgment.

I believe one reason the Lord told Ezekiel to draw a map was so he would have it to refer to often and he would be able to follow God's instructions simply with step-by-step detail.

The prophet, Habakkuk, also tells us, "And the Lord answered me, and said, 'Write the vision, and engrave it so plainly upon tablets that every one who passes may be able to read [it easily and quickly] as he hastens by'" (Hab. 2:2 TAB).

Set Your Face toward it

Ezekiel was asked to set his face toward his city, Jerusalem (Ezek. 4:3). He had to do this in the spirit. As he looked at his map, I believe he saw more than the city and its gates, roads, borders and building structures. He saw what they represented. He could see the natural and the spiritual.

When he drew this map, he probably took note of the

cities and peoples who surrounded and touched the borders of Jerusalem. He was aware that some had come into the city, bringing various customs, philosophies, and practices that influenced God's chosen people.

I'm sure he must have known how many people lived in Jerusalem because God cared for each one. He probably marked where the people lived and worked, where it was crowded or sparsely populated. Ezekiel's map probably indicated where the markets and business districts were located.

It is likely that he gave special notice to the hardest hit crime areas. He knew where the rich and poor lived, where there were schools, jails, and where the sick were treated.

He may possibly have inscribed on the map the places of worship and prayer that had once been glorious with God's presence.

Ezekiel Had Ears to Hear

Ezekiel had a circumcised ear and therefore was able to hear clearly the very unusual directions from the Lord. He discovered that what God told him to do wasn't always acceptable to human understanding and reasoning or comfortable and convenient for himself or for others. However, being yielded to God, it was usual for Ezekiel to experience the unusual in his relationship with God. He would have very graphic visions of God's glory and holiness. The Lord gave him an ability to see into the realm of the Spirit with great prophetic insight and revelation of the state of his present and future generation.

A Word to Gifted Intercessors

Generally, those who function in the ministry gift of intercession are prophetic people. If you feel led to move in a certain direction from something you have received in prayer, a dream, or vision and have any question concerning the course of action, it is important to have confirmation from the Word of God and two or three people who are experienced intercessors and operate in wisdom and discernment.

Because Ezekiel was a very detailed person, he kept a dated record of his prophecies. It is a good habit to write down what God speaks to you when you ask Him for His plan of action in prayer. You can do this in a journal or prayer diary. Some people keep two: one for personal, devotional reasons, and a second one for spiritual warfare purposes. There is no chance of forgetting or confusing what God has instructed you to do if you write it down.

Ezekiel's Light in the Darkness

The watchman, Ezekiel, lived among the exiles who were oppressed with the sin of idolatry nationally and individually. The people defiled the secret place of temple worship. They were hard-hearted, hard-headed, filled with rebellion, pride and wickedness.

Yet, in the midst of it all, Ezekiel was so close to God that he was able to enter His heart, feel His concerns. Ezekiel mourned and travailed with crying and wailing for God's people. Many times as intercessors, this will be our experience as we are moved by God's emotions.

The Lord revealed His emotions and very own personal hurt in Ezekiel 6:9: "Then those of you who escape will remember Me among the nations where they are carried captive, because I was crushed by their adulterous heart which has departed from Me, and by their eyes, which play the harlot after their idols; they will loathe themselves for the evils which they committed in all their abominations."

186

Ezekiel Fed on the Word

The Word of the Lord came to the watchman, Ezekiel, and he ate the scrolls. Truly, God's Word is food, indeed. But it is also a weapon. We need to read it, digest it, and use it as a two-edged sword to resist the enemy, break his power and cut his influence where he has tried to take hold.

The hand of the Lord was strong upon Ezekiel. He felt God's touch. The Lord wants to touch us and empower us with His strength so we may be able to proclaim boldly the Word over our countries and cities in the midst of rejection and opposition.

When he beheld the magnificent and matchless glory of God, Ezekiel fell on his face. Humility, obedience, the holy and awesome fear of the Lord were his outstanding characteristics. In fact, I believe some of our greatest spiritual warfare weapons in this day are love, humility, and the fear of the Lord, which is the key to obedience. That is why the heavens opened to Ezekiel! The heavens will open for us when we are humble, fear and love the Lord.

Take a Tile, Draw a City

In Ezekiel 4:1, God instructed Ezekiel to draw a map of the city of Jerusalem.

This tile, clay tablet, or brick, as some translations say, was a common writing material for that day. It was two feet long, one foot wide and four inches thick. While still damp and soft, the tile was engraved with a stylus, which is a triangular needle-like marking device. Then it was sun-dried to make the inscriptions indelible.

This is a profound example in Scripture of how God helped Ezekiel prepare and work out strategy to accomplish His purposes by using a map as a spiritual tool.

Just think, the Lord had Ezekiel inscribe an indelible picture of the city of Jerusalem on a clay slab. Yet, His promise to them, as it is to all of us, was that the inhabitants would be inscribed on His hand with indelible ink. " 'Behold, I have indelibly imprinted (tattooed) a picture of you on the palm of each of My hands. O Zion, your walls are continually before Me' " (Isa. 49:16 TAB).

As You Pray over Maps

As you begin to pray over maps of your city, state, or country, your eyes will be opened to see the sin and strongholds that control the people. You may find yourself weeping with the bitter and compassionate tears of our Lord because you will realize that these are not just whole countries, cities, and people groups that our God is dealing with, they are special individuals for whom Jesus shed His precious blood.

Pray that the blindness will be removed from those God has burdened your heart for (2 Cor. 4:3-4). Pray that they will come to the knowledge and acceptance of the truth of the cross. Proclaim the blood of Jesus and Isaiah 49:16 (TAB), over the cities of your map.

Lean forward in the spirit, peer into the distance, and see the picture of your city or nation imprinted on each palm of Jesus' hands.

Names Are Important to God

Names of people and places and their meanings are important to God and can be significant and helpful in praying for people and over maps. Ezekiel's name means "God strengthens" or "God is strong." On a personal note, my first name is Patricia, which means "noble one." My middle name is Frances meaning "free one." And my last name, Chen, is the exact Hebrew spelling for "grace" and "favor," found in Genesis 6:8. With God's help, I pray the fulfillment of the meanings of my name in my life.

Our Commander-in-Chief has a personal name and it is Jesus. He has a title, The Christ, The Anointed One. It is only by His name and out of a personal relationship with Him that we can use this name with authority and anointing in prayer. His name is very precious and powerful. We must use this name with an awesome fear and respect as we pray for our cities and over maps:

But he who is joined to the Lord is one spirit with Him (1 Cor. 6:17).

"You are my King, O God; *Command victories* for Jacob. Through You we will push down our enemies; Through Your name we will trample those who rise up against us" (Ps. 44:4-5).

"And these signs will follow those who believe: in *My name* they will cast out demons; they will speak with new tongues" (Mark 16:17).

What's in Your City's Name?

Jerusalem means "founded peaceful," "city of peace," "foundation of peace," "secure habitation."

It was obvious during this time of history, Jerusalem was not a peaceful and secure place. It wasn't living up to its name from God's perspective. That is why it was God's and Ezekiel's heartbreak. Perhaps, this is the case with the area or even some of the people you are praying for. I urge you to research and discover the name of your city, and you may find some beautiful redeeming qualities in it.

Affirm your city's value in the spirit by praying with scriptures relevant to its meaning. For example, one scripture says, "Pray for the peace of Jerusalem: may peace be within your walls, and prosperity within your palaces"

(Ps. 122:6-7 NASB). Pray that your city will, "depart from evil, and do good; seek peace, and pursue it" (Ps. 34:14). Proclaim and declare that the Prince of Peace is over your Jerusalem" (Isa. 9:6).

Do "Background Checks"

I attend church in the city of Oakland, California, and live in the East Bay area. I was reared in the national capital of the United States, Washington, D.C. I have a love for cities. God still loves the cities, too.

I've only just begun to scratch the surface in research on the history and background of the city of Oakland. However, in its name, I find great hope as my faith is stirred and heightened! Let me show you what I mean.

Oakland was named for the oak trees or oak groves on the grassy coastal plain in 1852 by Horace W. Carpentier. Oakland became the city of refuge and safety for many who fled from San Francisco in the great 1906 earthquake. Oak lumber is very sturdy and used for multiple purposes in construction and furniture. Some species of oak produce acorns that are used for food for small game animals.

The word *oak* is treated as a proper name in Scripture and mentioned fifteen times in the Old Testament and three times in the New Testament. In biblical times, the oak signified strength, growth, and permanence. Whenever the oak failed, it represented complete and absolute disaster.

From Research to Wise Prayer

My prayer declarations over Oakland are taken from Jeremiah 17:7-8 and Isaiah 61:4. In the last few years, Oakland has suffered from inner-city decay, drought, earthquakes, and a severe fire in 1991 that devastated an entire area.

190

These same scriptures can be declared over your cities that have had similar experiences with fire, drought, depression, inner-city decay. Just insert the name of your city and declare:

Blessed is (name your city) [that] trusts in the Lord and whose hope is the Lord. For (———) shall be like a tree planted by the waters, which spreads out its roots by the river and will not fear when heat comes; but her leaf will be green, and (———) will not be anxious in a year of drought nor will cease from yielding fruit.

Then (———) shall rebuild the old ruins, (———) shall raise up the former devastations, and (———) shall repair the ruined cities, the desolations of many generations.

Through persistent and prevailing prayer, your city can become more prosperous and productive spiritually and materially.

Uncovering the Unseen

A good example of how acquiring knowledge of place-name meanings can be another tool in praying with power for your city is this:

The Oakland hills firestorm that occurred on October 20th, 1991 was one of the United States' worst disasters. It claimed twenty-five deaths, 150 injuries; it leveled homes, destroyed 2,000 acres of land, and cost more than $1.5 billion in damages.[1]

When I began to research the area where the fire storm raged, I discovered that it is called *encinal de temescal*, or, "the oak grove near the sweathouse." *Temescal*, or sweathouse, came into Spanish from the Mexican Aztec name. The Temescal region was named for a sweathouse in the neighborhood. The Ohlone Indians were the neighboring people in the Oakland-East Bay region.

A sweathouse was a tightly closed hut used in the

traditional life of many Indian groups in the Americas to practice a religious ritual for male purification and for health purposes in order to sweat out impurities and illness. This ritual was considered a cure-all.

The huts were built beside streams. Inside, a fire was made with very hot stones piled up. Members would ladle water onto the stones, creating steam.

Regarding the religious rite, the men would work up a sweat for cleansing by doing energetic dancing and singing loud howling songs. When they felt enough impurities had been removed from their bodies, they would call out and invoke the spirits from the underground to come and fill them where they had been emptied out by sweating. Then they would hurry out of the small, sealed opening to jump into the cold stream. They believed this rite took them to a new and higher level of attainment in their manhood, spirituality, and health.[2]

Unfortunately, sweat will only cleanse the pores; it is Jesus' blood cleanses the soul from sin.

There were logical, natural reasons for Oakland's terrible fire disaster. The area was tinder-dry with drought, and the fire was fanned by fifty-mile-an-hour winds. Yet, we may also need to consider some unseen possibilities in the spiritual realm.

Throughout Scripture, God spoke to His people by using "natural disasters." He spoke through Ezekiel concerning a drought, to get the people's attention.

Before Taking the Land . . .

Before Israel got involved in aggressive warfare, the leaders sought advice and counsel from God. Many times, the Lord spoke to them prophetically, with rich symbolism, such as He spoke to Ezekiel. God instructed Israel in His strategies and ways of doing successful battle. Israel

192

would pray, and, as needed, the people would fast and sacrifice to the Lord. They would cry out for His help when they realized that sometimes war was unavoidable (Judges 20:23, 27, 28; 1 Sam. 7:8, 9; 13:12; 14:37).

Research was important in Bible times. Spies were sent out first to collect information on the city and what the con-dition of their preparedness for war was before they would go into that nation or city and engage in any form of warfare (Num. 13:17-29). In fact, spies spent forty days searching out the condition of the Canaanites before the Israelites entered the land *after* God had told them it was theirs.

First the Plan, Then the Battle

Ezekiel 4:2 says to put siege-works against the city, that is, to lay siege against the evils and darkness that have oppressed and dominated the city and kept it from good. A "siege" is

1. The encirclement of a fortified place by an opposing armed force intending to take it, usually by blockade and bombardment.

2. Any continued endeavor to gain possession and over-come opposition. The word *siege* mentioned in Ezekiel 4:2, 3 means

A) (Verse 2) "hemming in," i.e. a mound (of besieg-ers); figuratively distress; besieged, bulwark, defense, fenced, fortress, stronghold, tower.

B) (Verse 3) "to cramp," i.e. confine, an adversary, assault, beset, bind (up), cast, distress, fashion, fortify, inclose, or lay siege.

First of all, I believe the Lord wants us to know that it was His idea to encircle first.

He is the one who sits and is enthroned above the earth and encircles it by His very existence and power (Isa.

40:22). God drew a circle (the earth) upon the face of the deep and walks around it (Prov. 8:27; Job 22:14). He, also, seeks those who will build a wall and encircle those who are in need and danger by standing in the gap with prayer power (Ezek. 22:30). They are called watchmen. We need to enclose and surround the fortified places with Holy Spirit inspired prayers.

Siege-Works Strategy

Here are some points to consider and questions to ask ourselves before doing siege works:

1. Our relationship—Are we walking in right relationship with Christ and others? Repentance and reconciliation are to be our life style.

2. Our readiness—Have we put on the armor of God (Eph. 6:10-18)? Have we counted the cost, and are we willing to be obedient and faithful (2 Tim. 2:3-4; Luke 14:23)?

3. Our research—Have we done our homework? Research is not always reading and library work. Most times, it is being still and waiting before the Lord in silence and listening for revelation from His mind (Ps. 25:3-5). God will help us identify the enemy and establish what his tactics are (1 Cor. 2:16).

4. Our recognition—Do we acknowledge the fact that Jesus is the Warrior and it is He who makes wars to cease (Ex. 15:3)? He has all power and authority and has graciously and trustfully given it to us (Matt. 28:18; Luke 10:19).

Using the Blockade in Warfare

The blockade is any blocking action designed to isolate an enemy and cut off communication and commerce with him. In any way possible, the besieging army first would cut off the water supply to the city. The water supply represents the main life source. Therefore, the spiritual blockade is binding and loosing:

> But no one can go into a strong man's house and ransack his household goods right and left and seize them as plunder, unless he first binds the strong man; then indeed he may [thoroughly] plunder his house (Mark 3:27 TAB).

> Whatever you forbid and declare to be improper and unlawful on earth must be what is already forbidden in heaven, and whatever you permit and declare proper and lawful on earth must be already permitted in heaven (Matt. 18:18 TAB).

> For the weapons of our warfare are not physical (weapons of flesh and blood), but they are mighty before God for the overthrow and destruction of strongholds. [In as much as we] refute arguments and theories and reasonings and every proud and lofty thing that sets itself up against the (true) knowledge of God; and we lead every thought and purpose away captive into the obedience of Christ, the Messiah, the Anointed One (2 Cor. 10:4-5 TAB).

Example: My City of Oakland

In spiritual warfare I *bind* powers of hell, darkness, evil, crime, and lawlessness, and I *loose* powers of heaven, light, good, peace, order, justice, and rule.

The enemy and his forces feed on spiritual wickedness. It is their food and water supply. We can cut off their supply by binding in Jesus' name his powers to control and influence an area. Then, we loose (allow, permit, free)

195

those who have been bound and chained, to be in a position to be healed and restored to health and wholeness.

Another blockade is the powerful blood of Jesus. Our example comes when, first, the besiegers would fortify their own camp against attack. The blood of Jesus is that fortification and covering of protection that keeps us hidden in Christ as we wage warfare against the enemy who is destroying our cities. The blood is not only our covering from sin, but our overcoming power in battle. We can plead Jesus' blood over a person, people, or nation.

It is our responsibility to *command* the enemy to stop his works against our towns, cities, and nations. This is what was meant in Ezekiel 4:2 when the prophet was told to "set camps against it also."

Encamping near a city was another form of blockade. The word *camp* comes from a root word meaning "to bend or curve." Here again, this encircling concept is emphasized. A military commander had his army encircle the enemy territory and camp in the order of their march and rank. He would demand surrender of the city putting down very severe conditions (1 Sam. 11:1-2).

The commander was not only strict in his conditions for surrender towards his enemy but also strict in his regulations for cleanliness for his army (Deut. 23: 9-14).

Spiritual Camping Lessons

1. Entire consecration and pure heart is essential while in warfare prayer (2 Tim. 2:4). We need to be freshly consecrated for the battle.

2. Although the camp was a temporary structure, it had all the accommodations necessary to live. We must be well prepared.

Even though you might be inconvenienced in praying throughout the night, nevertheless, pray for the felt needs the people have, as well as their soul's need. Remember, victory will come when you pray throughout the duration of the battle (Luke 18:1; Gal. 6:9).

3. The arrangement of the camp was in order of the warriors' march and rank. We must be willing to join forces. A prayer project needs many people to join the ranks and unite their hearts together. The emphasis of encircling symbolizes continuity and oneness (Matt. 18:19-29; Lev. 26: 7-8; Deut. 32:30). We must also be willing to receive contributions from other intercessors. Just as there are different levels of warfare and demonic powers, there are different levels of praying and prayer warriors. (Eph. 6:12, 18).

The Iron Wall of Separation

"Set it as an iron wall between you and the city" (Ezek. 4:3). For us, this iron wall becomes a blood boundary line that the enemy cannot break through or cross over. Just as the death angel could not cross the threshold of the homes of the Hebrew people who painted their doorposts with lamb's blood, (Ex. 12:21-23), Satan cannot cross where we plead that blood. There is strength and power in declaring the blood of Jesus (Col. 2:14; Lev. 17:11).

"And they overcame him by the blood of the Lamb and by the word of their testimony and they did not love their lives to the death" (Rev. 12:11).

Casting up a Mound

"Heap up a mound against it" (Ezek. 4:2). Praise, worship, and praying in tongues is like casting up a mound against the wall of a besieged city (Jude 20; 1 Cor. 14:15; 2 Tim. 1:6-7). In order to get the siege weapon against the wall and into action, a large heap of earth was cast up to build an incline. Sometimes, it was built almost half as high as the city wall itself. Archers and slingers would assail their missiles from the mound and from the roof of the tower that held the battering ram.

With swells of worship, praise, and praying in our heavenly language, we will see the enemy become confused and his plans thwarted. With great songs and shouts of deliverance and joy, we will see walls of sin come down. We will see victory.

The Bombardment

To bombard comes from a word meaning "to batter with a cannon." It means to attack with bombs or artillery, to shell, to attack with *word* or *speech*, to assail with missiles of any kind. Our greatest bombs, shells, or missile fire is the Word of God. Praying the Word as I have previously spoken about in the chapter is God's battering ram.

"Place battering rams against it all around" (Ezek. 4:2). When besieging a city, a battering ram was the weapon used to beat down its gates and walls and hurl missiles. Launched from a catapult, the ram was an iron pointed wood log that would swing horizontally back and forth against a wall or gate, held by ropes secured to the catapult's tower. Missiles weighed up to 300 pounds and the ram needed up to 200 men to move it. The iron pointed wood log would beat against the wall again and again, wearing down and weakening the structure, focusing on one point until the wall broke (2 Sam. 20:15; Ezek. 21:22).

One of the primary strategies of the enemy against God's people and those who concern them is recorded in Daniel 7:25. "And he will speak out against the Most High and *wear down* the saints of the Highest One" (NASB). Another scripture that reveals his primary strategy against *all* of mankind is in John 10:10, "The thief comes only to steal, and kill, and destroy." The enemy is constant, persistent, and relentless in speaking *his* words against God and His people and wearing them down.

How much more then, should we speak God's Word and sing songs of deliverance over our land again and again? They are our battering ram. We can use them again and again until we see a breach in the wall of deception, rebellion, and spiritual blindness.

Worship and praise:

"You are my hiding place; You shall preserve me from trouble; You shall surround me with songs of deliverance" (Ps. 32:7).

Israel's victory song:

"Then Israel sang this song: 'Spring up, O well! Sing to it! The well, which the leaders sank, which the nobles of the people dug, with the scepter and with their staffs'" (Num. 21:17-18 NASB).

Deborah's victory song:

"Hear, O kings; give ear, O rulers! I—to the Lord, I will sing, I will sing praises to the Lord, the God of Israel" (Judges 5:3 NASB).

Songs of Jehoshaphat's victory:

"Now when they began to sing and to praise, the Lord set ambushes against the people of Ammon, Moab, and Mount Seir, who had come against Judah; and they were defeated" (2 Chron. 20:22).

Songs of Victory at the Jericho Wall:

"Then it shall come to pass when they make a long blast with the ram's horn, and when you hear the sound of the trumpet, that all the people shall shout with a great shout; then the wall of the city will fall down flat. And the people shall go up every man straight before him" (Josh. 6:5).

Ezekiel, God's Watchman Warrior

Ezekiel did what God asked of him. As he set his face

toward Jerusalem, his face was harder than flint (Ezek. 3:8-9).

Take a tile.

Draw a map.

Set your face toward your city, your nation, your world.

DORIS RUTH OTT

"Because God called me to be an evangelist, I often spoke in Aglow meetings across the U.S. from 1976-79," says Doris Ott, who has participated in Aglow's leadership since 1977.

In 1980, Doris began traveling to Europe to help in Aglow's outreach work in Western European countries and in Yugoslavia. In 1988, she became Outreach Director of Eastern Europe.

Currently, she serves as Aglow's International Director of Eastern Europe and now travels to Russia and to newly opened countries in the former U.S.S.R.

Because her area of responsibility in Eastern Europe is in the pioneer stages, Doris is an eyewitness to prayer as the essential foundation that builds healthy groups and more outreaches. "Women receiving the vision for Aglow in their locality only begin to know each other as they pray together," she says. "The vision stays burning when they continue to pray together as the Holy Spirit leads them."

13

...

Jericho Praying*
(Praying Down Walls)

By Doris Ott

Walls, obstacles, other hindrances and impossible situations have all become opportunities in my life for our heavenly Father to act in a way so natural to Him, and so totally supernatural for me.

The first Jericho Wall I encountered separated me from God. It came tumbling down in my kitchen in Paso Robles, California, in October 1969. God's fathomless grace caused me to admit failure and say, "Jesus, I give up, come into my life."

I had been programmed from childhood to *never* give up, rather, to persist and push through like a bulldozer and

---

* Unless otherwise indicated, all Scripture references in this chapter are from the New International Bible (NIV).

always make the best of each circumstance. But the Holy Spirit partnered with me so I could speak these vital words of invitation. Miraculously, the walls erected in my mind and heart vanished and God's Presence expressed itself in peace, joy, and righteousness through the Holy Spirit, as Jesus took residence in my life.

Since that time I have learned that God always prepares us to overcome what is down the road. For example, the Holy Spirit used the lessons God taught me in the past to be a diving board so I could jump into the waters of Aglow outreach in Eastern Europe, not ankle, knee, or waist deep, but ". . . a river I could not cross because the water had risen and was deep enough to swim in—a river no one could cross" (Ezek. 47:5).

I'd like to share some of my Jericho Wall experiences in Eastern Europe and Russia with you, so that you might know God's miracle-working power in that part of the world today.

Preparation and Surprise

In 1979 at the Houston International Aglow Conference, I ran into Betty Lowe, the International Outreach Director for Europe. God had already begun to knit our hearts together for His purposes and now the promptings from within were, "Go and serve Betty in Europe, whatever the need is." For the next eight years I did just that, always staying in Europe longer and longer. Finally, Betty needed to return to the United States permanently because of ill health.

Totally unbeknownst to both of us, the Lord had been preparing me to take on the pioneer work of Aglow in Eastern Europe. In 1989 I accepted this new responsibility and challenge and moved to Berlin.

Over and over again, my command from God was to

"arise and go," always by "twos." "Be strong and coura-geous. Do not be terrified; do not be discouraged, for the Lord your God will be with you wherever you go" (Josh. 1:9).

Countless Jericho Walls needed to be prayed down in our adventurous journeys into the countries of the former Soviet Union. Without God's miraculous intervention over and over again, none of these trips would have been possible.

In March 1990, three of us in ministry who shared an apartment in Berlin, Frauke, Agneta, and I, traveled to Corsica for three weeks to have a summit meeting with our "Commander in Chief," to prepare us for the places and timing of our ministry ahead. In Corsica, our Father spoke very clearly that we would go to Russia, but the borders were still closed at that time, and visas hard to obtain.

We knew also that He was turning all our previous plans in Finland topsy-turvy. Meetings had been scheduled for western Finland. Instead, by God's command, we were to continue to eastern Finland although we hadn't made any previous contacts. During that time, Frauke, praying in the Spirit, heard a woman crying out in the spiritual realm, "If someone doesn't come to help me, I will end my life."

When we left Berlin for Finland, we faced a Jericho Wall much like Abraham did when he left his country not knowing where he would land. But God had key people at the meeting in Helsinki who invited us to eastern Finland. Arriving by bus, we were driven by a Finnish sister in the Lord to a rehabilitation center for alcoholics which she and her husband oversaw.

On the way there, she said suddenly, "Could we please make a detour to pray for a man who has been flat on his back for three weeks with a back injury?" The Holy Spirit

205

witnessed to our hearts that this was His errand.

As we entered the home and began to pray for the man, we noticed his wife was weeping. We discovered that she was expecting her fourth child and was terribly depressed. As we prayed for her, God revealed to us that the child in her womb was especially called by Him and would bring great peace and joy to many.

The young mother was transformed before our very eyes when she heard this. Later in the car the Finnish lady said, "I must share something with you." The young mother had just told her that thirty minutes before our arrival, she had cried out to the Lord what Frauke heard in the Spirit during her prayer weeks before, "If someone doesn't come to help me, I will take my life."

That evening, five Russian people attended the meeting in eastern Finland, and we were able to minister to them. One of them, Katya, invited us to Leningrad in October.

This was the key to opening the door in Russia for us.

On October 15th, 1990, Agneta and I arrived in Leningrad, (now St. Petersburg), a city of six million people. Within twenty-four hours, God gave us a special place in the hearts of a family of six, whom we had never met. We were given a closet-size room where their four children usually slept. What luxury! Slava, the father, repaired TV sets and witnessed to his clients one by one. The Lord miraculously had snatched him from death's door three years ago when he was stabbed five times by robbers. Galina, his wife, also experienced God's divine touch after delivering a stillborn child and hemorrhaging severely. In spite of their difficulties, this precious couple realized the call of God on their lives.

Galina invited women to their apartment for Christian ministry on two separate occasions, and some forty women came. This kind of meeting was entirely new to these women as the government had forbidden gatherings except for birthdays, weddings, and funerals.

One Russian pastor had told us ahead of time that the women were too busy to take time to minister to each other, but God had already gone ahead and disproved his theory.

God's Delays, Our "Tests"

We scheduled our next visit to Russia March 15th, 1991, but the authorities in Leningrad held our papers until March 25th. Another delay ensued. Then, in an *open* envelope, the papers arrived two weeks later in Helsinki and were shipped express to Berlin. You can imagine our great relief and joy when we had visas in hand on April 17th. Our departure by train took place May 9th, with over 100 kilos of literature and foodstuffs.

God's delays can sorely test us, but He promises us perseverance and that is exactly what we continue to need in these ministry opportunities. "Because you know that the testing of your faith develops perseverance. Perseverance must finish its work so that you may be mature and complete, not lacking anything" (Jas 1:3, 4).

Miracles from Leningrad to Krasnojarsk

When we arrived in Leningrad no one was there to pick us up. Miraculously, a man who helped us with our baggage just *happened* to lead us to an authority who knew the family we were to stay with and phoned them. This authority was a believer—in a city of six million!

For the next six days, we had to really persevere: this was the Jericho Wall we could easily have given up on. We were able to get a visa to Krasnojarsk in Siberia some 5,000 kilometers from Leningrad. An Aglow had been birthed in Krasnojarsk on December 24th, 1990, through a vision given to Elena, a Christian sister from that city, and the four women she prayed with during our last trip.

Amazingly, this city had just opened to foreigners the end of February. Through another miracle, the assistant chief of Aeroflot Airlines in Leningrad let us pay for our tickets in rubles, a total of about $50 for both of us instead of $800.

On May 17th, 1991, the day set apart for prayer and fasting in Aglow world-wide, we flew to Siberia, four time zones from Leningrad. The nine days spent in Siberia were like nine weeks packed with excitement and activity, often more than eighteen hours a day.

Setting the Prisoners Free

Over and over again the thought came to Agneta and me to go to the women's prison in that city, but no one had ever been allowed to enter. Still, Elena and another Christian sister went two days—all day—to talk with officials. Finally, on the third day, perseverance brought the Jericho Wall down. We were unexpectedly led into a courtroom of 120 KGB officials. For over an hour they addressed us with questions and we were able to testify freely to a living God whom we had seen transform lives and Who gave the vision of Aglow for the entire world.

Miraculously, we saw those hardened KGB officials change from a negative to a fully receptive attitude toward us.

Two days later, we were permitted to share for two-and-a-half hours with 200 of the 2,000 women prisoners; we were also able to pray with them individually. Some received Jesus and were filled with the Holy Spirit. Many were set free and healed by the power of the Holy Spirit. At this writing, some fifty women in this prison alone have received Jesus in their lives.

We realized then that God was raising up a hidden army

208

of women through this outreach which the Krasnojarsk Aglow leaders would continue. As these prisoners grow in grace and are released to return to their towns all over the Commonwealth of Independent States, or C.I.S. countries as they're called in the new Russia, they will be lights in the darkness, burning with the Spirit.

Still, God wasn't finished with His miracles in Siberian prisons.

The Lord gave Galina from Krasnojarsk a vision for prison and women prisoners, the gigantic outworkings of which we still haven't seen the end of! God showed her that fabrics and sewing machines would be sent from the West to Krasnojarsk, so that the former prisoners who had become believers could learn sewing skills, earn income from sewn items that would be sold, and thus purchase train tickets to their hometowns in the C.I.S.

Even though we believed Galina's vision and held to the scripture that "Even on my servants, both men and women, I will pour out My Spirit in those days" (Joel 2:29), we had a few minor challenges: No factory, no sewing machines, no fabrics, no human way to get any of these.

How would this Jericho Wall come down, we wondered?

The Prison Vision Goes to the USA

First, God used an Aglow sister in the USA to spread the fire of this vision in the hearts of Aglow women who are part of Operation Link-Up Partners, a group who undergird projects such as this world-wide through intercession, networking, and financial aid. These women lugged ninety-seven boxes of fabric and sewing accessories to the 1991 Aglow International Conference in Orlando, Florida, USA. From there, the miracle continued as European Aglow people carried forty-five of these boxes back to Europe with them, delivering them to Frankfurt,

Germany. The fifty-seven boxes that were left behind had to be prayed through.

For awhile, it seemed as if they were immovable objects. Nevertheless, God had us persevere in prayer and obedience to His voice. Almost one year later the remaining boxes of fabric were transported to Sweden on their way to Siberia.

Meanwhile in Berlin, God gave a pastor a burden for this mission to prisoners and he investigated the purchase of industrial sewing machines: A sewing factory in Leipzig, East Germany, which had disbanded operation sold him twenty machines including operating instructions in the Russian language, and a factory outlet in Moscow for parts needed!

In June 1992 a Christian organization called A.C.V., (Action Committee for Persecuted Christians) transported the machines and fabric all the way to Krasnojarsk. God has wonderfully engineered this labor of love from the West.

He has also worked miracles in Krasnojarsk to make this sewing project a reality. The local Aglow leaders found a building to house the former prisoners as well as a place to install the sewing machines and set up a small store to sell the finished items.

Even the prison authorities donated thirty beds and sixty sets of bed linens for these former inmates now living in the sewing facility. The women in prison, who have such limited funds, collected money to buy the mattresses.

As I write this chapter, God is still working miracles for the prisoners. For example, the cost of buying this facility is three million rubles, impossible in man's eyes, but altogether possible with God. We are waiting to see how this Jericho Wall is finally leveled.

Lord, We Need Another Miracle . . .

"Lord, make a way where there is no way. We need a miracle just now." How many times we prayed the above words on our May 7th to June 15th, 1992, journey into Russia and Siberia. Jericho Walls loomed in front of us before we left Germany. For weeks we played a game of booking flights to cities within the C.I.S. only to have the travel agency phone repeatedly that another flight had been cancelled due to closed airports and fuel shortages.

The only booked flight left was the one from Berlin to Moscow and back. But even this flight was in jeopardy as the whole country of Germany was in the midst of a transportation strike. Intercessors at Aglow Headquarters in Seattle, Washington, U.S.A., Operation Link-Up Partners, and Aglow intercessors in Great Britain were alerted to pray for a way for us to fly in.

On May 7th, the very day we needed to leave, the Berlin airport opened. Coincidence? Absolutely not.

Still more obstacles stood in the way: the airport was open, but no aircraft or crew were available. Then, one-and-a-half hours later, both were ready to carry twenty passengers to Moscow. Lufthansa Airlines became part of the miracle in granting us permission to fly with 225 kilos (495 pounds) of humanitarian aid that was completely free of any baggage charge.

Supernatural intervention continued in Moscow as our ten huge pieces of luggage were waived through the "nothing to declare" lane, when all around us, officials scrutinized each and every bag of fellow passengers. It also "happened" that a nationwide pastors' conference was scheduled May 13th in Moscow which meant that all the food stuffs and clothing could be routed with each of them to the cities we designated.

211

To Leningrad and Beyond

On July 17th, 1992, we found ourselves airborne again from Berlin to Leningrad. God's open door in Russia was now going to take us to Moscow. In Leningrad we visited again with Slava and Galina, who were grounding a new church with several other couples.

Among our myriad appointments in Leningrad was an important meeting with a local pastor. We traveled one-and-one-half hours to his house and arrived fifteen minutes early but discovered to our disappointment that this gentleman had already left for the day.

We did not know that God was ready to level an impossible Jericho Wall minutes later. As we were leaving, two women approached us and introduced themselves. Genya and Nadya live in Vorkuta, 2,000 kilometers north of Moscow near the Barents and Kara Seas.

When we told them we represented Women's Aglow Fellowship, they were utterly shocked! We soon learned that they had just prayed that the Lord would bring someone from Aglow across their path, because they had heard about Women's Aglow Fellowship, International, at a Christian crusade. Before the evening was over, we had an invitation to Vorkuta, and Genya was burning with the vision of Aglow to reach the women of her city.

That same eventful day after boarding a bus, the lady sitting next to me began speaking English. Nina, a university English teacher had toured California, USA, in 1989 as a representative of the Soviet American Friendship Society. It was not long before I could share with her the reality of Jesus in my life and my purpose for being in Moscow. Nina invited Agneta and me to her apartment and her parting words were, "This has been an act of divine providence."

212

Jericho Praying (Praying Down Walls)

One week later we were sitting in Nina's living room, treated like royalty. Four hours hardly sufficed to satiate the spiritual hunger in this dear woman and her friend, Vera, who joined us.

A Space Where None Exists

A tremendous Jericho Wall—lack of space to live and breathe decently—is the dilemma of masses in the C.I.S. Available apartments are a rarity and married couples usually live with parents and grandparents until their second child is born. Lumilla, several times our hostess in Moscow, sacrificially makes available her humble two-room apartment to as many as sixteen people overnight.

Agneta and I were more deeply impressed with the need for space as we found ourselves part of a Russian Aglow delegation of nine, accommodated in two rooms for two weeks in the heat of summer.

It pressed us to pray earnestly that God would make way for an apartment where individual believers, especially those in leadership, could come to seek the Lord. Miracle of miracles, God placed in our hands the opportunity to rent a furnished apartment in Moscow for fifteen months.

Mikhail and Tanya, owners of the apartment, are not yet believers but have a hunger for God in their hearts. As we shared with them why we wanted the apartment, Tanya told us that one day before we first came to see the apartment in Moscow, the kitchen window was open and a white dove flew in, settled on the kitchen table, ate from her hand, and flew away at the end of the day. Again, one day before we came to rent the apartment, the same incident took place with another white dove in her kitchen. Somehow she knew of the spiritual significance attached to those events. I know God saw the plight of His people

213

in Russia who are so crowded for space: "For the eyes of the Lord range throughout the earth to strengthen those whose hearts are fully committed to Him (2 Chronicles 16:9). He has now made available to them an "alone" apartment where we can receive rest and refreshing in His presence during our times of intense ministry.

God Works from Greece to Bulgaria

In May 1990, Winifred Ascroft, Great Britain Aglow's national president, and I were gathered with the Greek Aglow ladies in a sunny corner of an outdoor restaurant in Thessaloniki. We were planning a program for that week and were in the midst of praying when one lady mentioned that we could very inexpensively take a bus to Sofia, Bulgaria, for two days.

Something went "click" inside.

None of us wanted merely a sightseeing trip without an opportunity to minister to Bulgarian women. The Jericho Wall we faced was not having a planned agenda for this journey.

As we gathered in a Greek home for a Bible study, Maria, a border guard between Greece and Bulgaria, offered to treat us to a cup of coffee as we crossed the border into Bulgaria the next morning. She also gave us the phone number of a believer in Sofia.

When we arrived in Sofia and contacted the believer, Pastor Josef was summoned and all five of us crammed in his tiny vehicle. He dropped us off near the city center and invited us to come back to the church at 6 P.M. for an evening service. Again, we prayed, "Lead us Holy Spirit so we can minister to someone." At 6 P.M. we entered the outer court of the church and were drawn to a woman standing nearby. Her name was Magdalena and she spoke some English. Soon her husband was by her side and escorted us into a tiny office where virtually all the leaders of the Pentecostal union were chatting. Imagine our surprise when we discovered that for the first time in forty years—on this very day—these pastors and their wives were gathering for a conference in Bulgaria.

"Would you speak to our wives tomorrow morning?" they asked. You can imagine how elated we all were and the next morning we poured out our hearts for three hours to a room crammed full of women with hungry hearts. One pastor's wife stood up with tears streaming down her face and said, "Yesterday, we cried out to God, 'The men have someone ministering to them, please send someone to us.'" We became the answer to that prayer.

Several months later, two of us made plans to go back to Bulgaria. We had learned that the economic crisis was severe: only bread and salt were available in the shops. Electricity was available only three hours a day but no heat.

The day before we were to leave for Bulgaria, our contact person hadn't replied. We tried faxing another contact with no luck. By 3 P.M. we were literally on our knees to find out if God was telling us *not* to go. The thought came to contact my son-in-law, Jeff, at a Bible school in Germany. Earlier in the year, I had met a Bulgarian couple who were studying there.

Within minutes, what had been a thick Jericho Wall, now seemed like a piece of thin paper. Stephan, the Bulgarian Bible student, had phoned his father who pastors in Burgas on the Black Sea, and the father said, "Come! You can preach Sunday A.M. and P.M. at my church." We were delighted with his invitation and were able to reach the travel agency to book the last flight from Sofia to Burgas just before they closed for the day.

Dependency on God demands absolute flexibility at all

215

times, but what fruit results. In eleven days we had twenty-one meetings. We experienced a total "first" at one of the gatherings. No one was present to translate so we relied totally on the gifts of the Holy Spirit and God transformed lives before our very eyes without verbal communication in a mutually understood language. Our God is truly a God of the impossible.

One woman came to the meeting heavily weighted with sorrow and grief. She had led some sixty people to the Lord in a small village and for three years she ministered to them. Then tragedy struck. Her son-in-law murdered her daughter and granddaughter and drowned himself.

God met her in such an awesome way that day in Bulgaria. We saw Him comfort her with His comfort and heal her broken heart. By the power of the Holy Spirit, her sacrifice of praise became a love song to Jesus and she was radiant with joy. She stayed three hours in the church and came again in the evening. She plans to minister again to her little flock; having been restored by our heavenly Father Who loves her so dearly.

A Miraculous Exit from Bulgaria

It took a miracle to get us into Bulgaria and it took a miracle to get us back out. While we were there, the nation went on strike and no flights were available. Worse yet, no one knew when the strike would be settled. Would it be one day? A week? A month or longer?

On Thursday, November 29th, a small group of Christian sisters in Burgas believed God for a miracle in this crisis. Two hours later, the head of the Bulgarian parliament resigned and the people handling transportation agreed to go back to work. Another Jericho Wall caved in! God proved Himself faithful.

Miraculous Healings in Romania

Our journeys to Romania involved many a Jericho Wall as we planned a trip for July 5th-10th, 1990. Before we left, our pastor in Berlin, Peter Dippl, prayed for us and offered these words, "You will go out as sheep among wolves but fear not. Your Shepherd goes before you and sends His angels to protect you."

When we arrived in Bucharest, we were cheated in an official money exchange at the airport. After that, we were approached by numerous suspicious looking characters who wanted to taxi us to our destination. We discovered that we were experiencing much confusion and were not able to her the Lord's voice sovereignly—neither through each other nor by His Word.

Immediately, we spent many hours crying out to the Lord to recruit intercessors for us. At last, the heavens opened and there was communication again.

Pastor John arranged to have a women's meeting for us in his church in Galati where the first Aglow outreach took place. We had expected about thirty women that evening. Instead, we watched in shock as some 400 packed themselves into the sanctuary by 6:30 P.M.

The needs of the women were so great that we needed a sovereign word from the Lord. The word turned out to be the whole chapter of Isaiah 35, which Pastor John's wife, Emilia, read aloud. As each verse was spoken, it fit the needs of a particular woman or child, and miracles began to unfold.

A grandma brought her deaf and mute daughter and grandbaby. She was riddled with fear that the baby would also be deaf and dumb. The stone-like fear rolled off her heart just as a fountain of joy erupted on her face. Verses 1-4 of Isaiah 35 came into fulfillment. She headed home immediately and phoned her good tidings around and still more women streamed in even after 11 P.M. Many mothers came with blind, deaf, mute, and crippled children and Jesus touched them.

Women in Ministry?

Pastor Jacob, who assisted Pastor John was skeptical of women ministering. That same night his wife experienced heart failure and was on the verge of going to the hospital. But God healed her totally. As a direct result of his wife's miracle, Jacob let us lay hands on his deaf ear and it opened up perfectly.

After midnight a young woman stood before us having absolutely no life emanating from her countenance. One of a family of fifteen children, her divorced parents had abandoned her and she had repeatedly attempted suicide.

Because every other woman sitting in that church had such tremendous needs herself, at first there was no compassion for one another. But as we ministered for a time to this one very needy soul, those around her began to pray and lay hands on her, and the Lord quickened life where there was only death. We all rejoiced as streams flowed in a desert (Isa. 35:6).

By 1:30 A.M. we left the church only to be led to a small room adjacent to the church where an eight-year-old girl had been brought, crippled from birth. For the very first time she moved one leg and both legs were lengthened before our eyes.

Several months later at an Aglow conference in this church, another Jericho Wall was lowered in a unique way in behalf of an individual life.

One Christian sister in a wheelchair had come to the meetings in the depths of depression. Three years previous, she had been run over by a tram and one leg was totally smashed. Several hours later a crane used to hoist the tram accidentally dropped it, crushing her other leg. During the conference, the Lord gave this precious one a crown of beauty for ashes! She was "aglow" when heaven broke across her countenance.

The next day Pastor John found out that a church in London was willing to cover this Christian sister's travel expenses to Great Britain and pay the costs of artificial legs for her. How faithful our God is in His own unique way.

Power in Yugoslavia

In Yugoslavia the Lord worked through a prophetic prayer to bring into being the first Aglow.

Yugoslavians Ksenia Sabo and her husband Victor had visited England in 1982. At an Aglow meeting, she received a prophetic word that she would coordinate women's ministry in her country. At that time, Ksenia was the busy mother of two toddlers.

Several summers ago, the couple had visited an Aglow meeting in Wales. There, the Holy Spirit began prompting Ksenia to start an Aglow Fellowship in Subotica. Within hours, an Aglow sister said to her, "I believe Women's Aglow is the answer for the women in Yugoslavia." This calling burned in Ksenia's heart so much that she hardly slept nights until she began praying weekly with four other women and searching for a meeting place.

By faith, they sent out invitations for a September meeting but had to cancel for lack of a place to gather the women. Undaunted by this setback, they set a new date for October 11th. Suddenly, Ksenia realized her birthday was on that day. "Father," she prayed, "if I really received a vision from you to start Aglow in Subotica, then let the Aglow meeting be my birthday present."

One week before the meeting, a restaurant in the center

of the city announced the addition of a room suitable for receptions; it would be free of charge to Aglow with the purchase of coffee and a small dessert per person.

Another miracle took place in an eastern block country when twenty women came together at that restaurant—Ksenia's birthday gift from God!

At one of the Subotica Aglow meetings a woman's coat was stolen. She called the police, who made charges against the hotel. The hotel manager, in turn, told Ksenia that Aglow would need to meet elsewhere from then on. But the Aglow women prayed and felt God asking them to buy the woman a new coat. This act of obedience reopened the door for meetings at the hotel. God also returned more money to the women than they gave away.

God's plans continue to unfold in the midst of war in Yugoslavia.

Now, Victor and Ksenia pastor a church in Senta. Victor's dream for revival was realized as night after night during the summer months of 1992, young people repented and were converted in street meetings. Now he plans to start a Bible school in which these young believers can be grounded in the Word and trained.

Judith's Miraculous Journey to Jesus

Judith had taken her whole vacation in 1991 to read the Bible, her hunger was so great. But she didn't know Jesus personally at that time.

That year Judith was diagnosed with a tumor on her colon. On Friday, June 19th, 1992, she had surgery to remove the tumor without anesthesia. The medical staff had exhausted their supplies in the hospitals in Subotica and Senta, due to the war. Her pain was so excruciating, she could only groan like an animal.

The very next day someone invited her to an Aglow

conference held for Yugoslav women in Millstatt, Austria. It was a twelve-hour journey. In the natural this was impossible, but she had an intense desire to go. It just so happened there was one seat empty next to her on the bus and she could sleep the whole way. When she arrived in Millstatt twelve hours later, she had absolutely no pain and all bodily functions, including her appetite, were normal!

During the week, she discovered Jesus as her personal Savior, and afterward, her countenance radiated the love of Jesus. She wanted to witness to all who would listen.

Times of Specific Strategy

Sometimes the Holy Spirit gives specific strategy in spiritual warfare and the outworkings are visible afterwards. Such a work of the Spirit took place in Innsbruck, Austria, as fourteen of us, carrying banners, gathered around a table decked with a map of that country. "We will shout for joy when you are victorious and will lift up our banners in the name of the Lord" (Ps. 20:5 NIV).

As we prayed, a strategy unfolded: a candle was lit for each of the nine provinces and nine specifically chosen songs of praise came forth. With the obedience, came such a confidence that God is stirring hearts in a new way in this nation.

During the first Austrian Aglow conference, March 27th-29th, 1992, we saw the fruit of the previous spiritual warfare. Some 300 people gathered, not only from Austria, but from the neighboring countries of Poland, Czechoslovakia, Germany, and Yugoslavia as well.

A Wall Down in Poland

Going the extra mile brought down a Jericho Wall in Poland. It was at the end of a back-to-back full schedule of ministry that a still small voice said from within, "Will you go the extra mile for Me?"

When I think what we could have missed so easily. . . .

We had an invitation to minister in the town of Zabkowice, more commonly known as Frankenstein. Americans and Europeans know its dark history: It was named after the fictional character, Dr. Frankenstein, the subject of a book and several horror movies.

Nevertheless, Jesus was there. Marek and Mariola, who pastor a little flock of forty people, live in the humblest of circumstances in Frankenstein. Yet contentment radiates from both of them. Sunday morning, church was held on the ground floor of their home. So hungry for the word of God was that congregation that fifteen people stood for three-and-a-half hours on a cement floor while the rest sat on chairs.

Our Father worked a beautiful miracle in behalf of Marek and Mariola's congregation, through a women's prayer-and-share group in Berlin. One woman, Hannelore, found a Lutheran pastor who just happened to have forty extra church chairs he wanted to donate. A relative of hers had carpet to cover the cement floor.

So on October 29th, 1991, two vans pulled out of Berlin "manned" by four women and one man, carrying precious cargo: church chairs, carpet, furniture, clothing, and food. When the vans arrived six hours later, they totally surprised Marek and his flock. Tears flowed freely as they expressed thanks to God, Who had heard their many cries for months.

Since then, personal relationships have formed between Marek's church in Frankenstein and our church in Berlin. Marek's wife, Mariola, received the vision to start an Aglow group in her city. How easy it would have been to ignore this "extra mile" nudge.

The Massive Jericho Wall Around Albania

A huge Jericho Wall stood around the country of Albania, and God has used a single, solitary woman to help penetrate this wall. Her name is Igballa and God sovereignly put us on the same conference grounds in Holland during February 1991.

Igballa was converted six years ago and was part of a church of forty in Kosovo, Yugoslavia. All these converts were of Moslem background. Forty years ago, two million Albanians were arbitrarily put within Yugoslav borders as a new Albanian boundary was made. Igballa's mother has been cut off from her family in all that time because of the changed boundaries.

Igballa had lost her job at a T.V. station and prayed, "Lord, what would you have me do?" He prompted her to approach several Albanian men and offer to teach their wives to read so they, in turn, could teach the children. The men readily agreed. Illiteracy is rampant among the Albanians, especially the women. As Igballa began going from home to home where groups of women gathered, she was able to pray with them and include portions of Scripture in her reading lessons. All was miraculously accepted. Then the borders opened briefly and Igballa took part in a crusade in Tirana, Albania. Because of this activity, she could no longer reenter Kosovo in Yugoslavia.

But God had His plan chartered for this courageous little fireball. In October 1991 she moved to Tirana to pastor a flock of new converts. This church now has 700 members. Igballa, in the spirit of Joshua and Caleb, did not see the giants in the land, only the abundant fruit that God had already prepared.

How to Face Your Jerichos

Every time we face a Jericho Wall it seems to be something we cannot penetrate, a total impossibility. "Now Jericho was tightly shut up because of the Israelites. No one went out and no one came in" (Josh. 6:1).

But it is totally possible for God. What does He say? "Then the Lord said to Joshua, 'See, I have delivered Jericho into your hands along with its king and its fighting men.'" God's promises are Yea and Amen—they are sure. But there are conditions for us to fulfill. It takes absolute obedience to do what God requests. Often those steps of obedience jolt our logic, our common sense. Would you have jumped to attention to the following mandates (Josh. 6:3-5):

1. March around the city once with all the armed men
2. Do this every day for six days
3. Have seven priests carry trumpets of rams' horns in front of the ark
4. On the seventh day, march around the city seven times with the priests blowing the trumpets
5. When you hear them, sound a long blast on the trumpets, then have all the people give a loud shout?

It takes a childlike faith and trust in absolute surrender to God to operate under His battle plan. What happens when we trust His plan, sometimes over our own common sense? In each and every impossible situation, "the wall of the city will collapse and the people will go up, every man straight in" (Josh. 6:5).

The victory is the Lord's and the glory belongs to Him. And ours is the inheritance He has promised us.

A BACKGROUND ON CIVIL WAR IN SRI LANKA

EDITOR'S NOTE: Civil war is a growing global problem, as strife engulfs many of the world's nations.

Since 1983, there has been war in Sri Lanka between the Liberation Tigers of Tamil Eelam (who are demanding a separate state), and the army of the Sinhalese-dominated Sri Lankan government. On May 1st, 1993, Sri Lankan President Ranasinghe Premadasa was assassinated during a May Day parade. The suicide bomber also killed twenty-four others and wounded thirty-six.[1]

This island democracy off the southern coast of India, boasts an eighty-eight percent literacy rate, nine universities, and one of the highest standards of living in Asia.[2]

It is a multicultural nation: the Sinhalese have a majority of seventy-two percent, the Tamils with twenty-one percent, and Muslims and others comprise seven percent of the population.

Thousands of lives have been lost and villages burned and destroyed due to this ten-year battle that rages in the North of the island, causing many problems to the law-abiding people living in this beautiful country.

---

1. Associated Press article in *The Seattle Times*, May 3, 1993.
2. Brian Hunter, Editor, *The Statesman's Year-Book, 1992-93* (New York, St. Martin's Press, 129th edition, 1992), pp. 1221-1228.

SYLVIA WEERASINGHE

In 1979, Sylvia Weerasinghe was a founding member of Aglow in Sri Lanka. She has served as Aglow's national president for Sri Lanka since January 21st, 1980, with oversight to forming new Aglow fellowships, developing ministry oppportunities, and establishing national Aglow conventions in her country. Since 1983, Sri Lanka has been under the siege of a civil war.

Sylvia was named foreign field representative for two years, from 1983-85, and currently is a member of the National Advisory Council, a position she has held since 1991.

"My vision of Aglow women at prayer is that through this ministry, women can be prayed for and reached; thereby Aglow fellowships will grow," she says.

In a stunning personal example of the power of God, Sylvia remembers a day long ago when she decided to take her life. "I felt I should give God a chance to speak to me before doing so," she recalls. "As I prayed, the Lord led me to read Isaiah 54 from the fourth verse onwards. That day I accepted the Lord and my life was transformed."

14

• • •

Prayer and Evangelism in War

By Sylvia Weerasinghe

On August 4th, 1990, the terrorists in Sri Lanka proclaimed a curfew. Shops were closed, government offices and schools were closed and transport came to a standstill.

Aglow's national conference had been going on for two days at the Hotel Galadari Meridian, and a terrorist curfew would not deter us. We knew the power of prayer and reached out to touch the source that could make the impossible possible.

That day the mostly non-Christian hotel staff were amazed at the courage we Christians had. Instead of quiet, the hotel auditorium swelled with nearly 800 worshippers praising God. Many sang to the Lord with uplifted hands, a unique gesture for most Sri Lankan Christians. But this,

229

after all, was a unique day.

Earlier, all the conference attendees who had vehicles brought as many people as they could to the conference hall; others found their way to the auditorium in difficult modes of transport or by foot.

All around the hotel, the city was dead, and some who lived in fear expected the delegates and the speakers to be attacked. Not for a moment did we move about stealthily or talk in whispers; we sang and praised God, we shook the place with hallelujahs and praise the Lord's.

That day, the Lord poured out His blessings in great measure upon all who gathered.

The speakers who came from abroad gave inspiring messages that were better than those given on the non-curfew days of the conference. Both men and women left the hall for their homes still experiencing the power of prayer. We realized with fresh insight that we can overcome the spiritual forces that wage war, simply by praying and watching its power defeat the enemy.

Power in Prayer

There is power in prayer. Prison doors can be flung wide open. We can stand in the midst of fire and not be burned. Lions can encircle us and we can be saved from their jaws. We can be protected in the midst of a civil war. Prayer can bring down the mountains that we face.

Day after day prayer can be a source of power through which we can face the battles that confront us from within and without. It can break the chains that fettered us; it can alter our lives completely.

God wants us to call upon Him in times of trouble. Even when we feel we have nothing to thank Him for, we can still praise and thank Him with a joy that comes from Christ in us.

Prayer is a powerful weapon to overcome Satan's

strategies. Often, we face problems, trials, disasters, and illnesses that can bring about depression, loss of faith, and a fear of the inevitable.

We try to overcome these emotions, sometimes temporarily or over a long period of time, but overcoming them in our own stamina may leave us feeling unhappy and discontented. We can still live in constant fear of the future.

How can we overcome then? The key is to know the power of prayer. First, God has not given us a spirit of fear (2 Tim. 1:7). Prayer is a powerful weapon to overcome Satan's strategies. Satan becomes a defeated foe, over and over again in our lives. The Lord leads us in the battle against the evil forces that surround us all the time.

It is in times such as these that I find enormous comfort in the secret place of prayer.

In the secret place of prayer we can meet our heavenly Father and experience His power and protection. He is our shelter in the time of storm. We can see many victories won as we battle with those who want to overcome us. Proverbs 18:10 says,

The name of the Lord is a strong tower;
The righteous run to it and are safe.

In the secret place of prayer, we recognize the awesomeness of Almighty God and know with spiritual certainty that He is able to do anything and everything. When we come before an Almighty God who is pure and merciful, we enter into His presence with the awareness that He also holy. Acknowledging His power, we humble ourselves before Him, and pour out from the depths of our hearts all that is hidden from the outside, aware that He is there waiting patiently to hear us tell Him what is within our hearts.

231

Strangers at My Door

I had an opportunity to practice being safe in the secret place of prayer during the height of terrorist activities in an area close to my home. The government had warned citizens to be careful and not to open the doors to strangers or entertain them.

It was dusk, and I was all alone in my home when I heard a knock on the door. Forgetting the warnings that had been given, I opened the door. I was surprised to see two stalwart, strange looking men standing by my door. Immediately I silently began to pray in tongues, and then asked them why they had come. While they were speaking I continued to pray in tongues.

They said they had come to ask me to be the chief guest at a Buddhist ceremony. I sensed that what they were saying was not true, that they had come with some other intention. I continued to pray silently in my spiritual language as I listened to them. God prompted my memory with the scripture that the power (Jesus Christ) that is within me is greater than he that is in the world. When they paused for an answer, I told them boldly that I could not do so as I was a Christian.

They continued to listen to me intently as I spoke to them about the living God I worship and that He knows the intents of our hearts, as well as our thoughts. They continued to listen as I gave them more of the gospel. I told them, too, that I would not bow down and worship any priest or image.

What a sense of relief came over me as they said they understood!

Then they requested some money from me. I knew that it was not safe to keep the door open while I went into my room to get some cash. Instead, I asked them to come back on another day. In the meantime, I told them I would pray and ask the Lord how much I should give them. They thanked me and walked away. I shut the door and praised God, realizing that we are more than conquerors in Christ Jesus.

Those two men never returned.

In God's Hands

God has shown me so many times, in so many ways that we are secure in His hands, as our urgent priority becomes prayer for our nation and evangelism—winning our people to the love of Jesus Christ.

If we trust in Him, the impossible can be made possible by Him—Him alone. Faith and prayer work miracles.

Humility in Prayer

God hears our prayers when we come into His presence with a humble heart.

In the sixth chapter of Matthew, Jesus spoke about how to pray. He illustrated this in Luke 18:10-14. by showing how two men prayed: One of them confessed humbly that he was a sinner, while the other proudly told God about all the good things he accomplished. Whose prayer was heard? The man who confessed his inadequacy. That is what Jesus said.

The disciples asked Jesus to teach them how to pray. We read about this in Luke 11:1-4. Promptly Jesus taught them the prayer we call The Lord's Prayer, the living example of God's way to pray: Recognizing God as our Father, praising and worshipping Him, confessing our sins so that His forgiveness can cleanse us anew, knowing that His will is best, asking His protection from temptations, calling on His name for deliverence from evil, and ending with the promise of His glory for eternity.

The Armor of God in War

God makes us able to realize His power no matter what situation we face, whether it is war, terrorism, famine or drought. We face evil forces all the time and it is the power of prayer that can bring down the strongholds and overcome attacks of the enemy.

In his letter to the Ephesians, Paul speaks of our putting on the armor of God.

> For we do not wrestle against flesh and blood, But against principalities, against powers, against the rulers of the darkness of this age, against spiritual hosts of wickedness in the heavenly places (Eph. 6:12).

In moments when we face grave situations, sudden illness, a problem that crops up unexpectedly, we can immediately pray to Him in faith.

> But let him ask in faith, with no doubting, for he who doubts is like a wave of the sea driven and tossed by the wind. For let not that man suppose that he will receive anything from the Lord (Jas. 1:6, 7).

I have seen in my own life how the enemy has fled with his weapons of fear and depression with which he tried to attack me. He was not successful as I withstood him in prayer.

In 2 Corinthians 10:3-5, Paul tells the Corinthians,

> For though we walk in the flesh, we do not war according to the flesh. For the weapons of our warfare are not carnal but mighty in God for pulling down strongholds, casting down arguments and every

high thing that exalts itself against the knowledge of God, bringing every thought into captivity to the obedience of Christ.

Many a spiritual battle is won on our knees as we go to Him in prayer.

Evangelism During War

In our war torn Sri Lanka, the Lord has raised up men and women who spread the gospel in areas where they have never heard the name of Jesus. Many have turned to the Lord and accepted Christ as their personal Savior due to the testimonies and messages they have heard and the miracles they have seen.

Though there is much freedom in my country, still there are people openly oppose Christianity and therefore there are persecutions.

But no human hands can stop the work the Lord has begun.

Recently, my sister-in-Christ Chitra DeMel and I went up to Hatton to conduct seminars. We have five WAFs in that area. At the seminar, many non-Christians accepted the Lord. One non-Christian couple came at night for prayer. I gave them the gospel of Jesus Christ and both husband and wife accepted Him. Another non-Christian lady who came for prayer, also accepted Jesus as her personal Savior. I believe their households also will be saved.

In remote areas in Sri Lanka, there is a thirst for the knowledge of Jesus. I should say there is an awakening in the hearts of the people. As the gospel continues to spread, there is also opposition and people are faced with danger.

Hindrances to Prayer

God's Word states that we can be hindered in prayer

either by asking for things that are not in God's will for us, or by not realizing that the Holy Spirit can actually help us to pray.

James tells us that the prayers of a righteous man avail much (Jas. 5:16). This is proof that we walk uprightly and live a clean and pure life. Jesus has set out standards for us to live up to. Therefore it is necessary first to examine ourselves, and be willing to exchange the evil for the good. To give up those things that are a stumbling block to our spiritual growth. James says,

> You ask and do not receive, because you ask amiss, that you may spend it on your own pleasures (Jas. 4:3).

Then how do we pray so that God will hear and answer our prayer? Jesus tells us that He is the vine and we are the branches. He says that if we abide in Him and His words abide in us, then whatever we ask from Him, we will receive (John 15:5, 7).

It means then that we must live a life that is pleasing to Him and then we will know how to effectively receive answers to prayer. Jesus emphasizes over and over again that we must abide by His words.

Our lifestyle must change completely; we must live, think, and speak in the manner He would want us to, giving up those things that are a stumbling block to our spiritual growth. Unless we read His Word daily, seek His face continuously, and enter into that secret place, we may not be able to see our prayers answered.

When we find it difficult to pray, God reminds us of His Holy Spirit.

> Likewise the Spirit also helps us in our weaknesses. For we do not know what we should pray for as we

ought, but the Spirit Himself makes intercession for us with groanings which cannot be uttered (Rom. 8:26).

How to Receive Answers

When we abide in the Lord, a transformation takes place within us. No longer do we want our will, but we happily surrender our will to His. When we pray we can tell Him the desires of our hearts, but also say, "Nevertheless, Lord let it be Your will." Peace follows as we surrender our all to Him in prayer.

There are many instances in the Bible where God heard and answered prayer during times of war. In 2 Chronicles 20, the Moabites and the Ammorites together were planning to attack Israel's King Jehoshaphat. He knew the secret of how to face this great danger.

First, he sought God's face. He began to worship God and proclaim His great power. He recalled all that God had done in the past and that they would seek His help.

The second thing he did was to place before the Lord the threats of the war they were facing. He brought all his fears and frailties before God. He also showed his dependence only on the Lord. God heard his prayer of faith, and Jehoshaphat withstood the attacks of his enemies.

Jehoshaphat allowed God to fight his battle. After his victory, he went home from the battle front rejoicing.

Jehoshaphat knew the sovereignty of the Almighty God. In Him was the power to give and to withhold. He realized the omnipotence of God, as well as His mercy and compassion.

How can we receive answers to our prayers? We must be still and know that God is God. We need to recall all His goodness to us and be mindful of the fact that He only can answer our prayer according to His will. His will is the best.

Women of Prayer

He has already forgiven us at the cross whenever we come before Him to confess our sins and repent. After we leave our burdens with Him, we rejoice and thank Him for what He is going to do. Then we leave His sanctuary of prayer with the assurance that He has heard and that He loves us with an everlasting love.

IQBAL MASSEY

In 1976 in Iran, Iqbal Massey began her own prayer ministry among women and believed the Lord for more than 2,000 prayer groups and hundreds of prayer chains and Bible studies among women in many Middle Eastern nations.

With prayer and evangelism as her life's mission, it is no wonder that Iqbal is the first Aglow International Field Consultant for the Middle East. This new position in Aglow reflects its concentration on prayer/evangelism for predominently Islamic nations. "If we are ever to reach the Muslim woman, it has to be from the committed and trained Christian national woman," she says.

Born in Pakistan, Iqbal came to know the Lord as a young woman in college. She and her husband Kundan, a graduate of Fuller Seminary in Pasadena, California, and well-respected teacher/evangelist, have served on the staff of Campus Crusade for Christ for thirty-two years. During this time, they lived and ministered in the Philippines, Iran, and Cypress as well as the United States.

Since 1991, she has represented the Muslim world on the AD 2000 and Beyond committee and co-leads the Middle East prayer track for the committee with Dr. C. Peter Wagner.

She and her husband have one adult son and one grand-daughter.

15

...

Praying for the Muslim World

By Iqbal Massey

The newspaper headline sent a shiver down my spine: "Blood Will Be Ankle Deep." On this wintry December morning in 1978 as I sat at the breakfast table in Tehran, Iran, I read on, "The streets are predicted to be ankle deep in blood as the next demonstration opposing the Shah takes place on Saturday." This was only three days away.

I sat transfixed with fear at the thought of what might happen on the streets just outside my door. I was alone in a country to which we had come three years prior to serve God. My husband and son were traveling in Beirut, Lebanon, which likewise had its share of political upheaval.

In a desperate whimper, I let out a cry to the Lord for help. I began to pray. While on my knees, I felt a compelling motivation, a seemingly audible voice, urging me to start a prayer chain. But how could I do this? The Islamic Revolution in Iran at that time had caused our church to be shut down. Most of the people with whom I regularly prayed had long since fled.

Now the city was run by bands of armed gunmen, who summarily executed those who did not condone the revolution against the Shah. At night the sounds of rapid gunfire and the vociferous chanting of "Allah-hoo-Akbar" (God Is Great) and "Marg baar America" (Death to America) permeated the air.

I got up from my knees, still not quite sure of how to initiate the prayer chain. I took a step toward the telephone, (which worked only intermittently), and promptly stumbled over a step, fell down, and injured my back. As I lay on the floor in pain—helpless—a thousand thoughts raced through my mind. How was I going to get help? Whom could I call if I made it to the phone? The twenty-four-hour curfew placed on the city made me wonder how I could get to a doctor.

I cried to the Lord to reach down with his healing hand and touch my back. I lay there praying for hours. At 3 P.M. the healing hand of the Father touched me. A wave of warmth and an electrifying power welled up inside me. I had been healed and by then I also knew what had to be done.

By 6 P.M. I was on the phone to anyone I could think of. To my utter amazement, God had prepared the hearts of all those that I called; they were all willing to fast and pray. Moreover, God kept the phone line operative during the entire time I was placing calls. I got in touch with a total of sixty believers, all of whom were Iranian Christians. A prayer chain had been initiated!

At about 11 P.M., I reached for the phone one last time to place a call to my husband, but the phone was dead.

God had kept it working just long enough for me to get through to the people on the prayer chain. He certainly does work in mysterious ways.

Prayer Moves the Hand of God

Three days later the demonstration took place. Over one-and-a-half million radical Muslims turned out on the streets to call for the overthrow of the Shah of Iran. The large majority had brought all manner of weapons with them, including machine guns looted from the local armories. Long speeches were given by Mullahs (Muslim priests), calling for the violent destruction of anything or anyone who might hinder the creation of an Islamic state.

Although there had been brutal violence in prior demonstrations, on this day not a finger was lifted in anger. The vast multitude of people assembled peaceably and then, at the end of the day, dispersed. Sixty Christians had been on their knees praying for this miracle. The awesome power of the peace of God saturated that enormous assembly and undoubtedly saved hundreds of lives.

From that day forward, the power of prayer has become a bottomless resource for me.

Changes and Challenges

We live in a thrilling time. The political and socio-economic scenarios of the world are transforming quickly. The dramatic political changes that we are witnessing contribute to an unprecedented need for urgent world evangelism. Iran, which was only a few years ago lenient toward the proclamation of the gospel, now is a fundamentalist Islamic state shunning all attempts by believers to preach the gospel.

On the other hand, the destruction of the Berlin Wall and the crumbling of Communism in the Soviet Republics, are unique historic opportunities for the Body of Christ to fulfill the Great Commission. Never before has ingress into these nations been as accessible. Muslim populations there number in the millions. As we witness these changes in the world, we are reminded of the words of our Lord in Matthew 24:33, "Just so, when you see all these things beginning to happen, you can know that my return is near, even at the doors" (TLB).

The March of Islam

Aside from the political changes that capture front page headlines, the changes that take place without headlines are the great challenge to the Christian church today. The greatest and most insidious of these is the global march of Islam and its phenomenal increase. In a spiritual "roll call" of all nations on earth, the Islamic world is identified as the largest unevangelized block, numbering by some estimates, in excess of one billion souls.

Someone described Islam as the Mount Everest of missions; it attracts much attention, but few climbers. Our mandate, given 2,000 years ago, is to conquer this peak and plant the flag of our Lord Jesus Christ upon it!

Challenge to the Church

The Islamic world is one of the last major challenges, missiologically speaking, to the Christian church. It will certainly be an instrumental player in God's plan for the end times and Christ's imminent return. In his book, *The Last of the Giants*, George Otis, Jr., describes three great strongholds of Satan's power that threaten the spread of the gospel in the final days. The three are: materialism, Hinduism, and Islam. Otis adds, "By far the strongest and most resurgent of these spiritual superpowers is Islam."

Make no mistake, the perspective and ultimate ambition

244

of Muslim leadership is to take control of the world by invading every segment of the world's people with the message of the Qur'an.

Today, Islam is one of the most dominating and fastest growing religions in the world, boasting a world-wide population of almost 1.9 billion.[1]

In recent years, Islam has experienced a resurgence of militant power with staggering effects. Its phenomenal growth, supported by the oil rich nations, has enabled Islam to cross its home boundaries and penetrate other parts of the world.

Islam U.S.A.

Once considered an Arab way of life alien to the Christian heritage of the United States, Islam is now poised to be a pervasive reality in America. It is estimated that six million Muslims live in the United States with the majority on the west coast. Now the third largest religion in the United States, by the end of this century it will place second.

Muslim communities in the United States have made great strides both politically and socially. Many areas have their own Muslim media networks. More than 1,000 mosques and Islamic centers exist today across North America. There are also scores of professional organizations dedicated to the proliferation of Islam within North America. Professor James Bill of Texas University postulates that over the next forty years the populist view of Islam will be the most important ideological force in the world.

The United Kingdom's Christian Handbook shows that while the Christian churches in Britain and Northern Ireland lose 100,000 members every year, Islam is expanding at a phenomenal rate.[2] The Muslim population there grew nearly 50,000 from 1987 to 1988. In addition, 300 British church buildings have been converted to mosques.

Understanding Islam

Christians in western nations need to understand the cultural chasm that separates the Western world from Islamic people, in order to intelligently pray for the Muslim world. God forbid that our lack of understanding of the cultural paradigms of Muslim nations could impede the spread of the gospel there. It is worthwhile to learn the basics of how and where Islam got its start because it is our mandate from above to see that the achievements of Islam do not continue. It is our obligation, responsibility, and assignment from above to pray unceasingly for the Muslim world.

Islam is the Arabic word which means "submission" or "surrendering to Allah (God)." Mohammed, the founder of Islam, was born in Mecca about 570 A.D. His father died before he was born, his mother when he was six years old. He was brought up by his uncle, Abu Talib.

The actual Muslim era started in 622 A.D. At that time, the Arabs were mostly animists, worshipping idols and believing in spirits. Mecca, the holy city for Muslims, was a well-known trading center for western Arabia. It was also a center of pilgrimage for Arab tribes throughout Arabia because of the famous shrine, the *Ka'ba*.

Mohammed married a widow named Khadija, whose wealth enabled him to have times of seclusion and prayer in a cave on Mount Hira. At age forty he began to see visions and was convinced that he was a prophet sent from God.

In the beginning, when Mohammed came in contact with Jews and Christians living in the land, he recognized the validity of both the Jewish and Christian religions and was greatly influenced by them. This is why we find several Old Testament stories in the pages of the *Qu'ran* (Koran). Additionally, he would face toward Jerusalem while praying, pray during certain times of the day, and

246

refrain from eating pork or strangled animals.

Later, when friction developed between Jews and Christians and the church was caught up in sins of compromise, prayerlessness, heresies, and divisiveness, Mohammed took advantage of the strife to set up his own religious practices according to the revelation that he believed had been given to him. He claimed that it was a renewal of the religion given to Abraham.

A Woman's Place in Islam

The Muslim world is a man's world, a male-dominated society.

Although there are notable exceptions, the average Muslim woman is a slave to her culture, her society, and especially to her religion. Islam is not just a religion, but a socio-political system which controls every facet of life. She lives, breathes, and has her being subject to a repressive, demanding, and all-encompassing force.

Islam does not have equal rights for women. A respected Algerian publication recently published an article stating the following, "God prefers men over women, because the latter are inferior." The author went on to state that the Qu'ran instructs the male to marry up to four wives, but the female to marry only one husband. A man also has the freedom to marry a Christian or a Jew, but a Muslim woman may only marry a Muslim.

The Qu'ran has sanctioned man's authority over a woman, shown by the quotations below:

Allah has not made man and woman identical, so it would be against nature to have total equality between a man and a woman (Surah 2:228).

And those you fear may be rebellious, admonish

them; banish them to their couches and beat them (Surah 4:38).

The Qu'ran further mandates that the Muslim woman be veiled and secluded. This seclusion involves two distinct parts: The first is a physical covering (a veil or a scarf); the second, a restriction to move about freely outside of her home. Many Muslim countries forbid a woman to drive a car, board an airplane, or check into a hotel without a male escort, who must be either her husband, brother, son, or father.

The Qu'ran states as follows:

Say to the believing woman that they cast down their eyes and guard their private parts . . . and let them cast down their veils over their bosoms and not reveal their adornment, save to their husbands (Surah 24:31-33).

That is why most Muslim women wear veils or long black robes. Recently, the resurgence of Islam has encouraged several Muslim countries to renew enforcement of the Muslim Shariah law which mandates that *all* women must be veiled while in public.

Socially and culturally speaking, a Muslim woman is restricted in her movements because she is perceived as a threat to the male ego. Islam has enshrined certain discriminatory practices and has devalued the worth of a woman.

In Islam, a woman's most important role and function is to bear children. Muslim men are extremely happy when a baby boy is born, but when a baby girl is born the men are often sad and angry because they must bear the burden of protecting her, finding her a husband, and providing a large dowry when she marries.

The Western world often wonders at the secluded and undervalued life of a Middle Eastern woman. However, after speaking personally with many hundreds of these women and interviewing them on this topic, I found most Muslim women to be satisfied and contented with their lives. Why? For these reasons:

1. They have blind faith and trust in the Qu'ran as literally dictated by God to the prophet Mohammed.

2. Their acceptance in their environment, group, or family is an important building block for Muslim women's self-image.

3. An extended family (number of children) gives them security and a sense of belonging.

4. In some settings, the structure of seclusion and veiling supports women's feeling of respectability, gives them security, and protects their femininity.

The Christian women nationals of the Muslim world are not exempt from the influence of Muslim society because they are subject to the same cultural limitations.

Behind the Veil, a True Story

To illustrate the day-to-day life of a Muslim woman, and to empathize with her plight, I want to share the following story.

Before you read the letter from Saida, it is important that you recognize that not all women in Muslim lands are subjected to the treatment described. Vast differences exist from urban areas to rural locales and from country to country. Nevertheless, this description is largely accurate for the majority of Muslim women who have yet to hear the gospel.

"As Reena a Christian girl entered the room, she saw her Muslim roommate, Salma, lying on her bed crying.

"'What's the matter?' Reena asked.

Sobbing bitterly, Salma held up the letter she had received from her sister. It read as follows:

Dear Salma,

Today my heart is broken. I wish I could talk with you personally, but this letter will have to do.

Salma, we are women in this repressive and demanding culture. We have no value or worth. According to the Qu'ran, we women are inferior to men. I have read in the Qu'ran where it says that, 'Men have authority over women, because Allah has made one superior to the other' (Surah 2:228). I have also read in Sahih Bukhari's book within a long dissertation regarding women that, 'Women are deficient in intelligence and in religion.'[7] Salma, what am I to do when this society condemns women and our religion declines us our rights? By now, you must be asking, "Why am I talking like this?"

Well, I remember our school days when we used to dream about the "Prince Charming," the "One and Only" that we would someday marry. When father chose Tarig for me, I began to put the face of Prince Charming with his name, even though I had never seen him.

After we got married, I thought that I would be living in some type of dream world. We came to live with Tariq's family, a very devout Muslim household. Almost everyone in the family prays five times a day. The men go to the mosque on Fridays, but the women are not allowed to go.

Salma, I am a prisoner in my own house. I cannot go out to visit or even telephone anyone without asking Tariq beforehand. Tariq wants to know about everything that I do, every moment of the day. I know that it is my duty to bear children and cook food, but it seems that Tariq is never appreciative, never satisfied. The other day I merely asked him where he had been and he replied, "Under the Holy book or the Hadith, I do not have to answer to you." Tariq demands things. He says that if I want to go to paradise when I die, then I must obey him. I am tired, not only physically, but emotionally and spiritually as well. I feel like just going away somewhere and asking God why? Why did You create women? Solely for the enjoyment of men?

My friend, Asma, gave me a Christian booklet, which I secretly read. The message made sense to me. However, I am frightened of the idea of becoming a Christian. The last Muslim wife that I knew who became a Christian was thrown out of her house and stabbed to death by her own brother, all because she chose to relinquish her faith in Islam. When I shared the contents of the Christian booklet with Tariq, he was furious and even hit me. What am I to do? I can't wait to see you.

Love,
Saida

"As Reena read the letter, she comforted Salma and told her that it is not only Muslim women who suffer this male domination, but Christian women in the Muslim culture as well. Reena went on to say, 'The one difference is that Christianity involves a personal relationship with Jesus Christ. It is not just a religion, but a relationship.' Salma was puzzled, but very interested in the words that Reena spoke."

The foregoing is meant to help one understand the difficulties involved in a woman changing her religious beliefs in a Muslim culture. Pray specifically for women who are subjected to this environment, that God will deliver them and that the gospel will reach them.

Our Prayer Challenge

"Ask of Me and I will give You the nations for your inheritance and the ends of the earth for Your possession" (Ps. 2:8).

The Muslim world is in dire need of intercession at this time in history. Muslims may pray five times a day but, they do not pray in the name of Jesus. Intercession is one of the most perfect forms of prayer. It is the one power on earth that commands the forces of heaven and is capable of destroying the walls of this Islamic Jericho. We need this supernatural force to combat the domination of Islam. My husband Kundan once said, "If we are ever going to reach the Muslim world for Christ, it has to be on our knees."

In our ministry to the Muslim world, the Lord spoke to me to begin a prayer and fasting program among the national Christian women. As a result of His blessing, literally hundreds of women got involved in the program. This in turn led to the unprecedented gathering of national Christian women from twenty-four Muslim countries for a seminar in Cyprus. These women were trained and given tools to begin their own prayer groups in their native lands.

The fruits of this meeting continue to flourish. Praise God, these prayer efforts have brought new trust, zeal, and commitment among the national believers and this fire is spreading as we see lives changed.

One of countless tangible results of this concerted prayer program is illustrated by the story of a governmental bureaucrat in a Muslim country. He announced that he was going to lead an effort to have a new law passed: anyone who denied Islam should suffer the death penalty. As months passed this man continued to push for this new law.

The Christians began an organized, concerted prayer effort. It seemed for awhile that this man would realize his ambition, but the believers never ceased praying. A few months later the newspaper headline proclaimed the news: the bureaucrat had been fired from his position. He no longer had the clout to get the law passed!

Another moving example of the power of prayer involves the dreaded secret police, part of many Muslim nations' governments. A national, Abid, returned to his country after attending a Christian conference abroad. Upon his return he was thoroughly searched at the airport. After an Arabic Bible was found in his luggage, he was interrogated for three hours, but they finally let him go.

The next day he heard a knock at the door. A stranger said he had heard that Abid had an Arabic Bible. He asked to see it, claiming he had never seen a Bible in his language before. When Abid placed the Bible in his hands, he begged to borrow it for two days.

The very next day Abid was arrested and falsely accused of witnessing (which is against the law). The secret police agent at Abid's door used his Bible as proof.

Under the Islamic law Abid was sentenced to death. The news spread rapidly within the small Christian community. For a full seven days, a program of prayer and fasting was carried out. One day before the scheduled execution, the file was brought before the judge to sign execution orders. As the judge looked over the case again, the Lord intervened. The execution order was changed to six months in prison at hard labor. Today, Abid is a radiant Christian.

How to Pray for the Muslim World

What can you personally do? Here are a few suggestions:

1. **Friday Fast** (Ezra 8:23)—Join with hundreds of others praying and fasting for the Muslim world on the first Friday of each month.

2. **Prayer Watch** (Isaiah 62:6-7)—Choose a Muslim country and set up a prayer watch in your prayer group for that nation.

3. **Prayer Walks** (Joshua 1:3)—Take a walk through the local battlefield—around mosques, churches, neighborhoods where Muslims live. The purpose is to pray and sprinkle the blood of Christ on the very area where the Holy Spirit's presence is needed.

4. **Prayer Siege** (2 Corinthians 4:4)—Travel with a group of believers to a Muslim stronghold (this could be a Muslim country or even a mosque in the U.S.), expressly to put a wall of prayer around that area. Claim the territory in the Name of Jesus.

5. **Prayer Travel on Your Knees** (Psalm 67:2)—Take a prayer trip to Muslim nations on your knees with a globe or an atlas. In addition, get out your encyclopedia and learn about these nations as you pray for them. On the map, lay your hands on each country as you lift it up to the Lord.

6. **Adopt a Muslim Nation** (Ezekiel 22:30)—Adopt a specific Muslim country as a Sunday School class or Bible study group. Learn all you can about that country. Pray for the unity of Spirit for the believers in that nation. Pray for the political leadership of that nation that they might see God.

7. **Prayer Partner** (Matthew 18:20)—Get in touch with a national believer from a Muslim land who lives in your country or abroad. Various mission organizations can help you locate a believer. (Note: If the believer is overseas you must be quite careful of what you write or say to him).

Pray with that person, encourage, and be a beacon of light to her.

When we face the awesome challenge of the Muslim world, it is also helpful to study the book of Acts to learn how the early church secured the supernatural power of the Holy Spirit to face and conquer the challenge of paganism in that era.

Specifics

Specifically, pray for the fledgling local church that exists in the Muslim world. God does His work through His own people. Pray that He will enable these believers to have the wisdom, boldness, and strength to present the gospel to their own people. Pray for the Christians that are at this very moment being persecuted both physically and mentally for their beliefs. New converts to Christ have been abducted and imprisoned and even martyred in Iran, Pakistan, Afghanistan, and other Muslim nations.

Yes, the Muslim world is a challenge, but certainly not one that is insurmountable in the Lord's power. Prayer moves the hand of God, which in turn can transform the world in an instant. Committed, praying Christians can change the destiny of a nation and most assuredly can speed Christ's message to the Muslim World.

It is my heart's conviction that if the Muslim women are ever to be reached with the gospel it must be through committed Christian women on their knees.

JANE HANSEN

Jane Hansen has served as international president of Women's Aglow Fellowship, International, since 1980.

Her association with this nondenominational ministry for women began a decade earlier in Edmonds, Washington, where she was elected president of a local fellowship. Later, she became vice-president of the Washington State Area Board, regional director, assistant to the international president, and international board secretary.

Jane's late father, Thomas Williamson, ministered in the Christian and Missionary Alliance church after emigrating to the United States from Ireland. Jane was born in Mount Vernon, Ohio.

She serves on several committees representing the Body of Christ including the U.S. Lausanne Committee and the International Advisory Council of the Lausanne Committee for World Evangelization, the U.S. Board of AD 2000 and Beyond Movement, the Spiritual Warfare Network, the International Charismatic Consultation on World Evangelization Advisory Council, the North American Renewal Service Committee (NARSC), the Association of International Mission Services (AIMS), the National Prayer Committee Board of Reference, and the March for Jesus U.S.A. National Advisory Board.

Because of the worldwide scope of Aglow's ministry, a large portion of Jane's time involves travel to many parts of the world. Her desire is to help women recognize the uniqueness of their design, their identity and value in

God, and their place of service in the Body of Christ. She feels the Aglow ministry is a special tool in God's hand, a "network of caring women," for "such a time as this." Her message to women is one of hope, healing, and restoration in Jesus Christ.

Jane and her husband Howard are the parents of three grown children and six grandchildren.

16

. . .

The Prayer Vision
of Aglow

By Jane Hansen

The year was 1980. I had just begun my term as president of Aglow.

Although I certainly had moments when I wondered if I were qualified to preside over a Christian women's organization that had fellowships in more than thirty nations, I was tremendously excited about the mission and thrust of Aglow's ministry.

Here was a world-wide organization dedicated to leading women to Jesus Christ, providing opportunities for them to grow in the power of the Holy Spirit, and minister to others. Clearly, the direction for Aglow had been established. Since Aglow's beginning in 1967, evangelism was its reason for being. In 1980 it was still Aglow's mission and first priority. I felt deeply honored to be part of this move of God.

Yet, during those early days in my new position, I often felt like a woman entering the living room of a new home. The colors were vibrant and fresh, the furniture restful and warmly inviting. Even the accent pieces, the pictures, and well-placed figurines blended beautifully with the color scheme. The whole room radiated comfort and peace. But for me, there was something missing.

Somehow I yearned for a fire that would bring life to the beautiful but unused brick fireplace of this imaginary home. A fire that would crackle and snap, one that would roar with warmth on a cold day and bring vitality into the room—and into the whole house.

Stirred to a "New Thing"

Isn't that often the way the Lord stirs us to a "new thing"? It's as if we can no longer be content with what has served us well in the past, as good and as fulfilling as it was. We become restless; we yearn for something more. God wants to take us forward.

One day, as I was rocking quietly in our little white kitchen rocker at home, I was consciously yearning for that "something more" in Aglow. "Lord," I asked, "what is on your heart now for this ministry?"

Only the sound of the chair, rhythmically moving backward and forward, filled the silence that followed my question. Yet God's love was tangibly present in the room as I rocked and sighed, comfortable in the warm and precious communion with the Lord.

A Network of Praying Women

Then, in the stillness of my heart, I heard the Father speak: "Aglow will be a network of praying, warring,

260

interceding women, covering the face of the earth." The strong impression was an unmistakable message though I did not audibly hear His words. And immediately, not in a vision but in a flash in my mind's eye, I saw a group of women praying.

I could see women from all around the world: African women praying in the bush country; Indian women dressed in saris praying in their homes; Chinese women praying as they walked along with their children; Russian women in the subways, praying as they sped to their jobs; Latin American women interceding between customers at their market stalls. I saw women of all races, colors, and creeds making a difference in their corner of the world.

The picture of the multitudes of praying women so overwhelmed me I audibly spoke out my astonishment there in the kitchen: "Lord, how could this be? Aglow is only in thirty-three nations?"

While I couldn't grasp the logistics of how the Lord would bring this about, I nevertheless could not deny the impact of His emphasis on my heart. It was so clear that there would be women from every continent of the world, from cities to remote villages and hamlets, from seemingly insignificant places, calling into being the very life and heart of God.

As if to assure me that I'd heard Him correctly, God brought to mind a scripture passage from Revelation describing those gathered at the Last Day: "Behold, a great multitude which no one could number, of all nations, tribes, peoples, and tongues, standing before the throne and before the Lamb" (Rev. 7:9).

I felt strongly impressed that Aglow would play a part in the actual fulfillment of this scripture.

The Net Is Stretched

It has been thirteen years since God shared His heart for prayer in Aglow with me. In the years between 1980 and 1989 Aglow experienced eighty percent of its growth, with fifty percent occurring between 1985 and 1989. Across every cultural and national barrier women were coming to Christ and fellowships were opening around the world. Prayer was making a difference.

The implementation began at every level of the organization. Soon the network of prayer took shape. Let me recap the highlights of its development.

In 1982 Aglow held its first prayer conference. In 1983 at our International Conference in Washington, D.C., 4,000 women from over fifty nations fanned out across the capital city of the United States. They went to the steps of the White House, to embassies, even to the ghettos—praying and doing spiritual warfare for the kingdom of God.

In 1990 a prayer thrust was launched with coordinators in all fifty states in the United States and over twenty other nations. From this has come several twenty-four-hour prayer watches held simultaneously around the world. Through this prayer thrust, we have taken Aglow women on two prayer journeys, one to Moscow, Russia, and one to Korea, where women have walked the land, praying and fasting.

In August 1992 we "cast a net of prayer" over the United States. Every state was covered from New York to California to Hawaii, from Alaska to Florida. Many of the women met at the borders of their states; others went along coastal areas, praying at seaports. The vast state of Alaska, for instance, was covered by land, sea, and air. A team of women visited every state capital, "planting" the Word of God in an appropriate place as a sign of claiming the government for the kingdom.

Testimonies Pour In

Women prayed and God answered. Exciting, thrilling, miraculous answers to prayer poured in. Lives were being changed as women met the Lord. Women were being healed. Families were restored. Communities were touched with reconciliation as women reached out in pregnancy clinics, schools, and hospitals to share the love of Jesus.

While I mention these events in the past tense, let me assure you the testimonies continue to pour in to International Headquarters. As you read the few I've shared below, I know your heart will be stirred in gratitude to our prayer-answering God.

• Tribal warfare had plagued an African Zulu village for years. An Aglow Bible study began in this remote area, the women learned how to pray God's Word, and soon tribal warfare ceased.

• Aglow women have driven and even walked through drug-infested areas of large cities, praying and interceding. They have seen housing units shut down as the "drug nets" were uncovered.

• Aglow women have reached out to prostitutes and drug addicts with the gospel. Their prayers have released hundreds from these addictive prisons.

• In drought-stricken areas of South Africa, Aglow women are assisting in the feeding of thousands of people, working together with other Christian groups to offer financial and food-gathering help.

• In Australia Aglow women have covered over 11,000 miles, on "treks" to reach the isolated women of the Outback with the gospel. Some areas are accessible only by light aircraft. Hours were spent praying and interceding for these women before and during the treks; many received Christ and were filled with the Holy Spirit. The Aglow women literally "plundered" the camps of the enemy, and they have seen the establishment of Aglow fellowships in the Outback. One lady they visited said, "With you ladies coming, it shows that God has not forgotten us out here."

• A group of Aglow women in Florida began praying, holding a Bible study, and doing acts of kindness inside a mental hospital where the "no-hope" chemically ill were put to await death. Out of the original 198 patients, 188 were either discharged or transferred to other wards after two years of Aglow ministry.

• At the 1991 International Conference, the nation of Cuba was prophetically called forth. In January 1993 a team of Jamaican Aglow women went in to "scout out the land." They found three Aglow fellowships had already started and six more were planned to begin soon.

• Aglow has come recently to Angola, Africa; to Mongolia; and to several areas of the former USSR.

The word the Lord spoke to me in 1980 seemed utterly impossible at the time. Yet, we have seen and are seeing the fulfillment of that word through women from every continent who give themselves to pray for the establishment of Christ's kingdom.

Women's Gift for Prayer

I am often asked, "Why do you think God uses women so significantly in the area of prayer?" To begin with, I believe women are uniquely designed by God to birth life, not only in the physical sense but in the spiritual realm as well. Women are by nature sensitive and intuitive.

In addition, they seem to carry the burden for their family's physical, emotional, and spiritual needs in a different way than men do. How many of us could say, "I wouldn't be here today if it were not for my mother's or my grandmother's prayers?"

The Woman Is the Enemy's Enemy

I believe there is a strong biblical explanation for women's involvement in prayer. We see it early in the book of Genesis where God describes how the woman, particularly, would play a part in undoing the effects of the Fall. "I will put enmity between you and the woman, and between your seed and her Seed; He shall bruise your head, and you shall bruise His heel" (Gen. 3:15).

The birth of Jesus perfectly fulfills this scripture, but there is an ongoing fulfillment as well. While Mary physically gave birth to Jesus, who on the cross ultimately crushed the head of Satan, so we as women, are uniquely designed to bring forth life in the spiritual realm.

In a very real way, we are the enemy's enemy. As we give birth to godly seed (through our prayers and intercessions), over and over again that seed takes its stand against God's enemy.

God Will Build His Church

I believe we are on the brink of a new move of God's Spirit on the earth. The roots of that new move are in the prayer He is bringing forth in His people. I believe we will witness in our lifetime a harvest of souls into the kingdom like nothing we have ever seen before. God is already bringing revival in specific places of the world.

Just this year, Aglow released the first Aglow prayer map which highlights the area of the European, African, and Asian continents that lie between 10- and 40-degrees latitude north of the equator. Christians involved in global intercession commonly refer to it as the "10/40 window."

Women of Prayer

The historical and biblical significance of this portion of the world is tremendous. It has long been a stronghold of Satan. The heart of three major religious blocks is located here: Islam, Buddhism, and Hinduism. Two-thirds of the world's people live here, and they are ninety-seven percent of the least evangelized people in the world.

What is more, part of the "10/40 window" covers the place where Jesus lived, died, and rose again. It is where He made His plan clear for mankind. It is the part of the world where the fall of man occurred and where Satan still maintains a stronghold. Many refer to it as the last stronghold. Even today, this geographical belt continues to resist the gospel.

When Jesus said, "I will build my church, and the gates of hell shall not prevail against it" (Matt. 16:18 KJV), it means that He will build His church in Iraq, Iran, Mongolia, and in every other resistant pocket of the world.

There is not a place of resistance in the earth that can withstand the penetration of the gospel of light. No geographical belt, no "10/40 window," no ghetto, no resistant pocket that He is unable to penetrate. God has declared it so. But He asks us to join with Him first in opening the way through prayer.

"Ask of Me, and I will give You the nations for Your inheritance, and the ends of the earth for Your possession" (Ps. 2:8). What a gracious and powerful invitation!

Strategic, targeted, united prayer in the whole Body of Christ is what God will use to bring forth the revival and the imminent harvest we are sensing.

What a privilege, what an honor, what a challenge He has entrusted to the ministry of Aglow. May He multiply our prayers for His kingdom and His glory.

Source Notes

The appearance of a book title in Aglow's source notes in no way constitutes a recommendation by Women's Aglow Fellowship, International, or the author. Occasionally an author may refer to or quote from another source as an example or to reinforce a point only.

CHAPTER FOUR

1. From a speech to the student body at Christ for the Nations, (September 1992).

2. *New Comprehensive Shilo English Hebrew Dictionary.* Compiled by Zevi Scharfenstein (New York, NY: Shilo Publishing House, 1973), pp. 295-296.

3. Jamie Buckingham, *The Nazarene* (Ann Arbor, MI: Servant Publications, 1991), p. 89.

CHAPTER SIX

1. Cindy Jacobs, *Possessing the Gates of the Enemy* (Grand Rapids, MI: Chosen Books, 1991), p. 100.

2. Edgardo Silvoso quote taken from a memorandum to supporters and friends on "Plan Resistencia," Sept. 15, 1990, p. 3.

3. Charles Ludwig, *Mother of an Army* (Minneapolis, MN: Bethany House Publishers, 1987), back cover notes.

4. Jane Hansen, *Women of Prayer* (Lynnwood, WA: Aglow Publications, 1993), p. 18.

5. Quin Sherrer and Ruthanne Garlock, *A Woman's Guide to Spiritual Warfare* (Ann Arbor, MI: Servant Publications, 1991), pp. 109, 110.

CHAPTER NINE

1. Francis MacNutt, *The Power to Heal* (Notre Dame, IN: Ave Maria Press, 1977), p. 39.

2. Ibid., p. 40.

CHAPTER ELEVEN

1. Dick Eastman, *No Easy Road* (Grand Rapids, MI: Baker Book House, 1978), p. 107.

2. Ibid., p. 108.

CHAPTER TWELVE

1. *San Ramon Valley Times*, Dec. 9, 1992.

2. Beth Bagwell, *Oakland—The Story of a City* (San Francisco, CA: Presidio, 1982).

CHAPTER FIFTEEN

1. George Otis, Jr., *The Last of the Giants* (Tarrytown, NY: Chosen Books, 1991), p. 61.

2. Ibid., p. 75.